The Face of Defeat

PALESTINIAN REFUGEES
AND GUERRILLAS

The Face of Defeat

PALESTINIAN REFUGEES AND GUERRILLAS

David Pryce-Jones

Holt, Rinehart and Winston

NEW YORK CHICAGO SAN FRANCISCO

Contents

When I tread the verge of Jordan,
Bid my anxious fears subside :
Death of death, and hell's destruction,
Land me safe on Canaan's side.

HYMNS ANCIENT AND MODERN

1 · Refugees

Finally the special flight took off for Tel Aviv, as the opening hours of the Six-Day War were drifting away. We passengers, by now fretful, were issued with a canvas-bound pocket book, *Readings From Holy Scriptures*, selected by the Chief Rabbi for the Jewish Members of HM Forces – remaindered, one might say, from a former crisis. On board, besides press correspondents, were panels of doctors from New York hospitals and a computer team from MIT. Also an Israeli star fresh from mastering Broadway, and he was kissed goodbye by an actress in a celebrity suit and sombrero. Their picture must have been in the papers. I sat next to a Canadian freelance demolition expert in some concocted uniform of his own on which were pinned the insignia of various armies – Tanzania, the Congo, Rhodesia. He stood up to join in when the Broadway star and his friends had a little sing-song going. We had heard the latest television commentary in which the typecast know-all young man from the Institute of Strategic Studies and a specialist on Middle East weaponry had declared that nobody should believe either side's statements about aeroplane losses. He had spoken of dog-fights to control the skies, and his menaces vaporized away only in the Mediterranean dawn, high and empty above a still shore. Landing alongside anti-aircraft guns by the runway, we clapped with relief, applauding ourselves perhaps.

No customs, no formalities. A shuttered city, its streets nakedly white in the freshening light. Sandbags in doorways. That the population, normally so busy, was absent gave an impression of waiting on events, for what might suddenly come round the corner. Here was the atmosphere of a pogrom, as described in literature. In Jerusalem at last there were soldiers and barriers at key points into the Old City, and the world's journalists clamouring for passes and jeeps from anybody who looked as if he might have authority. The Broadway star had been rushed up there like a secret weapon.

In spite of the hasty bulletins and hastier cables of a war like this, facts do get established in the end and make sense of the sequence of time-stopping sights in the present: of the little white flags, for instance, or scraps of linen rather, which were flying on the Arab houses, even the humblest, by the time we were able to form into some sort of group and cross the old Armistice Line into the West Bank. Here and there in the countryside were wandering Arabs. They paid no attention to us or to anyone. At King Solomon's Pool is an expanse of cool water, serene and landscaped. Next to it a tourist café is set in pretty gardens which were deserted until we swarmed round them. The till was untended and above it was a tractor calendar with a bosomy model. Four love birds had been abandoned in their cage. By the pool an Arab with the face of an elderly English colonel said, 'Some stay, some run away.' The sentence provided the basis for so many snap-judgments. As we stood there a family returned down the road, a teenage boy carrying his baby sister who had a skin disease and whose bare and dirty feet had been cut on the stones. Two women balanced their possessions on their head. 'We go back,' the teenager said. 'Welcome to our town.'

Farther on, at the entrance to Bethlehem, a welcome arch had already been erected in blue and white colours. A Jordanian car was carrying the Mayor of Bethlehem in his business suit to an appointment with the new military governor. By the road was a parked loudspeaker van. We were to be the first postwar visitors to the Church of the Holy Nativity. A shell had opened a hole in the roof. A dignitary introducing himself as the Archbishop of Pella stood near the damage amid a dozen Israelis in paratroop smocks, guns in hand. In the body of the church one of them echoingly operated a bolt-action. Outside, one member of our group, a famous war correspondent, excitement and drink at last too much for him, passed out, his head elegantly tilted against the car window. At Kfar Etzion, where General Dayan was arriving to mark the return to a place from which the Israelis had been driven out in 1948, he slept on. Through Hebron too, as strangely deserted as Tel Aviv had been, and where to one side was another loudspeaker van.

Back to Jerusalem on the road to the Garden of Gethsemane, and there the corpses began, Arab Legion soldiers stretched out on the pavement under grey blankets, dusty boots pointing up, British-style tin helmet a useless halo. I counted nine, one of them crouched in a corner of a garden almost under a balcony where an old man in a tarboosh was sitting impassive. Lorries were burnt out on the bends. A United Nations convoy swung by, the roof of its leading landrover riddled with bullet-holes. At the Mandelbaum Gate crowds of pious Jews were kept back from the Wailing Wall by iron pickets and mounted policemen. Through this drama of the living and the dead the international correspondent slept on in his drink. All the same, his dispatches proved to be the usual trouble-shooting stuff and for propaganda purposes are sometimes quoted as evidence. I used to think that this illustrated the frivolity of public opinion and the debasing manner of its formation by the mass media, but such may not be quite the case: no blind eye, no attitudinizing, make a bit of difference: there is a conflict and no outsider is party to it. Four years later, a few of those little white flags were still to be seen hanging limp in the sunshine, the houses still abandoned.

A reporter of events like these almost always feels himself to be in the wrong place, even if he is not. After Jerusalem and the West Bank had been taken, the fighting swung towards Syria. Through the open windows of the car blew the smell of burning grass. which scented that summer. Once in the Galilee, the military traffic became a solid jam for kilometres. During the night Syrian artillery continued shelling and next morning the tanks and half-tracks passed up the Golan Heights. A captain enjoying himself hugely in his jeep, gave me a lift, and spent the rest of the day trying to get supply columns to go in the right direction. We finished up at Maadabah, a Syrian base camp and a brown disconsolate place at the best of times. Two officers were making away with a car, having tied to its roof a dentist's drilling equipment antique enough for a museum, and some filing cabinets. A long while was to pass before I realized that the information in those files might well be what was most worth acquiring on that plateau. Meanwhile the sun had set below us, the moon was reflected in the Lake of Galilee, and suddenly all down the valley the electric lights came on after a week's black-out, in straight lines, in dots, like Morse.

The road south to Sinai follows a railway line on which the old Mandate officials used to travel up from Port Said. Their coaches would be rejoining the Orient Express at Istanbul. For days after the fighting cars which were crossing that single-line track at the bottom of the Gaza Strip had to pull out to avoid an Egyptian soldier spreadeagled on his back. Farther along towards the canal are frequent concrete water-holes supplied by a pipe-line from Egypt but which the Egyptians had turned off. At these regular points there was likely to be another corpse or two, often someone who had exchanged his uniform for pyjamas. In the desert were also the prisoners who had been collected; they sat in bell-tents or had been put to work digging in the sand at various places. They had learnt a few all-purpose words like Shalom and Welcome, and were eager to use them. At Kantara these prisoners were being returned home. Two Egyptians were running a launch, ferrying across loads of fifty men at a time. A complete register was kept by a Cairo doctor employed by the Red Crescent. On a table beside him lay the book, fat and tatty as an old telephone directory, with its lists of names written in English and Arabic. Unable to sign, the soldiers pressed their thumbs into a pad of indelible purple ink and made their mark on the page before moving over. On the West Bank four or five Egyptian officers sat in deckchairs with a view of this operation. Behind them a road was closed with barbed wire, fencing off an enormous throng of people who had come to look for their menfolk. The sun was beating down, the crowd was waiting with an absolute patience.

And you had to return, trip after consecutive trip, past that corpse by the railway track. Sometimes a couple of figures with a makeshift bier were slipping away through the Khan Yunis orange groves, probably afraid of being given orders. Decomposition was swelling the corpse and bursting its uniform, and in the process the legs were being compelled upwards, a few inches at first, then higher and higher, to end straight up in the air, in a mockery of the gesture of prayer. No smell of burning grass out here, but of rot, and with it came bluey and oily flies gorged out in that suffocating furnace. They settled round your eyes and face so thickly that you seemed to be slapping yourself. In spite of showers and clean clothes that odour of death stuck in the nostrils; it had some power of regenerating itself in the air-conditioned night among the telex messages, in the smartness of the hotels in full postwar swing with the opinion-makers from all over the world come to scavenge and boast.

In the week after the war Sheikh Ali Ja'abari, the Mayor of Hebron, held a press conference. Hebron was again more or less itself, unbolted and unshuttered, the soldiers gone from the Park Hotel, the Arab and Jewish holy places swarming with visitors. The market was open. In the offices of the Municipality chairs had been lined up for dozens of journalists. Sheikh Ali Ja'abari, venerable in white robes and a turban, is old enough to have seen the Israelis, the Hashemites, the British and the Turks before them, but he was nervous and so was his interpreter, an Israeli colonel. The Hebron notables sat at a table. First a pronouncement: the entire Arab world was to know that the Israeli army had not harmed the local population. Then in answer to questions he explained himself in more detail. One after another, each more pointedly, journalists asked him if he was not afraid of being a collaborator. To judge by some later reports of violence and a puppet mayor, some of these journalists might have been at a different town that day. And these were the very men who up till that moment had been generating unqualified victory sentiment on behalf of the Israelis.

Dupes or stooges, all of them, at the bidding of manipulators, one thinks for a moment, but actually they are doing their best by simply interpreting the event before them in the light of their own European or American experience. They are innocents abroad. What does collaboration mean to someone like Sheikh Ali Ja'abari as he witnesses his fourth conqueror? Everybody in Hebron recalls more than vividly how during the Mandate the Jews in the town were massacred, and as a result the Jewish community ceased to exist. Everybody in Hebron is more than aware that the turn of the Israelis has come. That press conference served as an insurance in case the Israelis were considering reprisals to repay old scores. So each fresh development of this Arab–Israeli situation carries with it a tangle of interests, a historical past and a calculation for several possible futures. Not much, if anything, may be taken at face value.

At that press conference Sheikh Ali Ja'abari must already have heard that two villages, Beit Awwa and Deir Mersin, on the Armistice Line not far from Hebron, had been in part destroyed by the Israelis. The desire to pre-empt further action of the kind in the area by praising the Israelis for their conduct so far prompted that press conference as much as the fear of massacre. Few others, if any, in that big room in the Municipality knew that there had been any such methodical destruction of buildings either during or after the war. But soon afterwards, thanks to one or two foreign consuls and some protesting Israelis (in particular Amos Kenan, a political columnist whose article on the subject boomeranged round the world) it was learnt that in addition to the two Hebron villages, three more in the Latrun area commanding the Jerusalem road – Beit Nuba, Yalu and Imwas – had been wholly razed. Also that one end of the small town of Kalkilya had been destroyed and 135 houses in Jerusalem bulldozed to provide access to the Wailing Wall.

Then again, this was not all as straightforward a matter of conquest as it might appear but derived from what had been left unconcluded and beyond negotiation in 1948. Since then, the Wailing Wall had been barred to Jews. From Kalkilya

Jordanian long-range artillery had been able to shell Tel Aviv, only a few kilometres away. Its fate had depended on a muddling series of orders and counter-orders between the local Israeli commander and his superiors. The Latrun villages had been the scene of fierce and repeated fighting because of their strategic positions. To destroy them supposed that the Israelis would be shortly withdrawing, as a consequence of some settlement, and did not want the Jordanian army to reoccupy them and dominate the Jerusalem road as before. There is no purpose in obliterating places which are to be kept. Indeed, the subsequent rebuilding of the Hebron villages and of Kalkilya has been used to argue that the Israelis are not making amends for mistakes, but annexing.

No sooner was the war over than it was shown to have no outcome, but to be characterizing itself once again as a refugee problem. Destruction of these villages might be, as the Arabs were saying, a preliminary to driving out altogether the inhabitants of the West Bank. Or it might be, as the Israelis were saying, that there was no policy of any kind for these eventualities, that officials and commanders were taking decisions locally in what had become unexpectedly a territory to administer, and sometimes they did well, sometimes badly. Counter-stories were being given substance before one's eyes. Only a few days before, whole families or groups with their possessions in bundles could have been observed on the roads, in the fields, coming and going, to be out of harm's way. Nobody molested them, they molested nobody. Radio Amman was reported to be telling West Bankers to stay where they were. As for the loudspeaker vans which I had seen, one of them with the Israeli entry into Bethlehem on 7 June had stopped at the crossroads near the Frères College. There the van had broadcast to the population that they should go on the road to Jericho or face the consequences. The mayor, Elias Bandak, was in his office with the Bethlehem and Beit Jala notables, and advised the population on the contrary to stay. During the course of that afternoon when we had glimpsed him and his party on their way to surrender, he had complained about the loudspeaker van and its broadcasts. Now Elias Bandak will take you to the balcony of his house (which is also Bandak's Furniture Factory and his office as honorary consul of Honduras) and from there will point out the crossroads and the van's position. It has been established to his satisfaction that the major in charge of that van was solely responsible for the broadcasts. Official inquiries have taken place, reprimands and apologies have been given. According to the mayor, fortunately less than one per cent of the town became refugees.

Atrocities, like a will-of-the-wisp, leaped ahead just out of reach: in such and such a village a massacre was declared to have taken place; young men of military age had been picked out for concentration camps and death; mass graves gaped in Gaza or in Jericho; the churches had been pillaged. Surprisingly no rapes. Usually the man with the information did not claim to have it first-hand but from a neighbour or a friend. There was no intrinsic reason for disbelief. A war between two such involved antagonists was likely to be punctuated by atrocities. When the stories concerned the shooting of civilians, I would ask someone to accompany me to whoever had told him. This person would refer to someone else who should have the facts – and so it would go on in a chain of credulity. That I was investigating was a spur towards substantiating whatever it might be by providing me out of kindness with what I was so plainly wanting.

These rumours were parables of defeat and they contained insights into the initial shock of Arabs confronted by Israelis, the unpredictable and unwelcome victors who might search their houses for arms, requisition their cars or summon them with orders to resume work. In the end I could unravel two of these rumour-chains into firm incidents (and both were already well publicized). The first was the death of the guardian of the Garden Tomb in Jerusalem, a cave so named by General Gordon of Khartoum in the supposition that Christ had been laid there after the crucifixion. The guardian, a local personality, had left this cave during the fighting but had walked into a burst of automatic fire. The second case concerned a man in Bethlehem who was mentally ill (in itself suspect, but his daughter who works for the British Council and Elias Bandak both confirmed it) and was shot at the window of his house while making gestures at the Israeli soldiers in the street below. Something like two hundred civilians, Arabs and Israelis, were killed during the fighting, mostly by artillery fire or by being caught up in the retreat of the Jordanian army, and probably months of hard work at the time could have validated each one.

President Nasser was supposed to be in an Israeli gaol, and a photograph of him bound hand and foot to have been published on the cover of a Saudi magazine, which was always sold out, though somebody somewhere had seen it. The war, then, had been organized by Saudi Arabia whose king had paid the Israelis a fabulous hoard of gold. King Hussein, meanwhile, had entered into a plot with the Israelis whereby he would allow them to occupy the West Bank for a token period. To this end he had issued blank ammunition to the army and had refused to do any real fighting (though wreckage could be observed all over the West Bank). Once Nasser had been toppled and the Palestinians had learnt their lesson, the Israelis would be fulfilling their part of the bargain and withdrawing. There were the English aircraft carriers about in the Gulf of course, and much more besides, full of imagination, really a form of folk-art.

Out of so much confusion propaganda has the outstanding function of providing a shape, something to hold on to. People have been told what to expect, they know what to do about it. Besides, they had been through this before. The refugees from the Six-Day War were a continuation of 1948, another of its unnaturally delayed reactions, like the destruction of the Latrun villages. In 1967 most of the refugees crossed the Allenby Bridge which is a few miles east of Jericho, spans the Jordan and carries the main road to Amman. Some thousand or more feet below sea level in the deep rift of the Jordan valley, the spot is always torrid, overpoweringly so. To stand there under the shade of some big willows in the slack heat with now and then a striped hornet humming around, as that exodus passed by, was to whip up the sensation of having been in the wrong place. It was essential to have stood farther back down the line, to re-trace the experience behind this futility which could lead only to more futility. A whole history was shuffling in the dusty path ahead, yet it was apparently beyond meaning and motive.

Last time, in 1948, plenty of witnesses had seen just such moments with similar women in these unsuitably beautiful dresses, and their children, and the universal bundle of blankets, a cooking pot, some food. What they wrote is brought to life only if it is convenient evidence that the Arabs were driven out physically by the Jews, or on the contrary were leaving for their own reasons and later invented excuses to regain self-respect and sympathy. Yet the claims and counter-claims of 1967 are as far beyond resolution as those of 1948. In the last resort, even present facts right there on the Allenby Bridge depended upon trust and mattered less than interpretations put upon them; indeed, facts like these may be immaterial to those who have to live them.

The bridge had been blown up by the retreating Jordanian army. The refugees had to step on its half-sunken girders or through shallows. There was a hubbub inspired not by panic but a sort of steadfast disorder. They were going to cross and they did cross. Half of them had already been refugees in 1948 and could not have expected much to result from this new flight. That fact alone, one would have thought, should have deterred anybody in 1967 from starting out as a new refugee – no good would come of it. To say so to them, to plunge in and grab out of the ruck anybody who looked as if he would be articulate, who might perhaps have the clue, was to lose bearings and give in to despair. The whole refugee problem, 1948 itself, the invisible key to local history, lay in the palm of the hand and slipped between the fingers. They stopped, they answered, they said the same few phrases, they stood in front of you, they looked, they moved on.

In some cases they had explanations: husbands or bread-winners were in other Arab countries and the families would be reunited over there; some did not want to live under the Jews; some had heard of the destruction of the Latrun villages and thought their turn would come. It was not that they were immediately afraid of the Israelis for as often as not they had met none until that very day. They were wholly intent about their own affairs. After all, in their numbers the refugees could easily have disarmed the handful of soldiers on duty at the bridge, and shot them before escaping the few yards into Jordan. It was the even-tempered quality of the procedure which was so baffling, an even-temperedness which was a refusal to respond to new circumstances. Some deeper collective impulse was at work. These refugees were retreating into what they knew, safely, choosing a future which would be like the past. These twenty long years they had rejected the Israeli reality and automatically they were continuing to reject it.

The Israelis, one saw, who came down to the bridge among these refugees, had perfectly well understood that this flight was the ultimate criticism which the Arabs could bring. Some of them did not mind in the least while others were out to show that there were no grounds for it. They behaved in uncharacteristic ways, either being tiresomely aloof, or else overkind, subservient about lifting luggage and children and accompanying the elderly. By the end of June, when the Arabs were still leaving in hundreds every day, the Israeli authorities were making them sign a paper that they were leaving of their own free will. If the Israelis permitted the refugees to trek on foot, they were accused of callous indifference, and when they provided transport they were accused of systematic eviction. Had they forbidden departures, they would have been tyrants. In such a position nothing they did could be right; they could neither explain nor apologize.

Though what is free will for people who are in the main illiterate and conditioned by inherited codes of behaviour, for whom traditions count for more than ideas? Going down to the bridge frequently you had the impression that if the Arabs did see the Israelis they did not register, they had closed their senses to them. Here was a face-to-face contact for which neither party was then ready.

Like everything else, the numbers of these refugees are

disputed. In 1961 the Jordanian government census gave the population on the West Bank as 730,000. The Israeli census in August and September 1967 showed 597,637 inhabitants of the West Bank and 65,857 residents of Arab Jerusalem. The yearly natural increase on the Jordanian figures had been compensated already before the war by steady emigration from the region. All in all, probably about 130,000 people crossed in 1967 from the West Bank to the East Bank, while another 70,000 came from the Gaza Strip. Some Arab estimates are higher, while UNRWA figures are the largest of all, in total up to 430,000, which suggests among other things that more than a quarter of the West Bankers became refugees. (On the Golan Heights, from which everybody except 6,000 Druzes fled, the estimates vary from 70,000 to 115,000.) Most of them were the less settled elements of the population, either those uprooted in 1948, peasants who were landless or had found a marginal existence by moving into towns and camps, or whose family members had already emigrated.

The established people of Jerusalem, Ramallah, Nablus, Hebron or Gaza, did not flee. Nor did the people of Kalkilya whose houses had been destroyed. They waited in the fields around until within a few days they were granted permission to return. They camped on the rubble, they salvaged what they could, they lived in tents, they petitioned the mayor and the Israelis, and they planned to build again. To visit the place was to expect outrage, the indignity of something wanton and admitted to be so. As so often in the Middle East, the experience was otherwise. The wrecked area looked like a builders' site in need of tidying up, not at all dramatic. There is so much poverty and misery around that a little more or a little less has to be finely gauged. The eye ceases to notice, and sensibility withers: the mind remains informative, but it relays the thought that in Kalkilya there are still many living in more degraded conditions than these poor people picking at smashed stones and mud bricks. Conscience rallies, though: the strong owe it to themselves never to treat the weak like this. And just then all such speculation is stopped, for a helicopter is arriving to deliver

General Dayan and three or four of his officers. As is his style, he swoops out of the sky like a Homeric god descending into the conflict of mortals. Probably the whole trip has been carefully pre-arranged but it looks like an improvisation, as if the great man wanted to see and hear for himself the cries for justice. He needs no badges of rank, for that eye-patch of his serves the purpose. A plain khaki shirt and trousers. He moves with a physical quiver of vitality and interest. Here comes the Mayor of Kalkilya, a natural aristocrat, old and erect and unhurried, followed by the notables. Children dart around, goats pull at tethers, the flaps of the tents open, and men and women stumble out, they crowd about. It would be the work of thirty seconds for them to take revenge by stoning to death the enemy general with the ruins of their own houses. But instead they are clapping him; he walks among prolonged applause. Well, says a dumb-founded Israeli, it's because Dayan has that special charisma of leadership, the virtue of *baraka* which Arabs so much admire. It's because he's a conqueror, a hero, he's all that they wanted Nasser to be. Common-sense tells one that they are grateful to be allowed back to Kalkilya, for they know that the majority of those across the river will stay there. Still, this clapping is excited, apparently genuine, and perhaps it was for themselves as well as for the general and his power. They would be remaking their lives right there on the Armistice Line and the clapping presaged the smashing of old stereotypes. It was a signal. Had it not been a little like that when we too had applauded at the end of our special flight, on the first day of the war, overcoming our own fear?

The polemic between Arabs and Israelis has by its nature to be both negative and positive, a martyrology as well as an epic. Each side must prove its victimization, while being blameless. Unable to afford the least chink, the national arguments range from what God and Abraham actually said to one another down to who should get the credit for the water-pump in Silwan village – and, most fundamental of all, to how the war of 1948 should be judged, for then the State of Israel and the Palestine refugee problem simultaneously began. The issue is still alive, it is not a matter for the record and may never be until it is as legendary as Moses's crossing of the Red Sea and the drowning of Pharaoh's chariots. Virtually everyone involved wants to show how little he could have done except what he did. Propaganda, which may nonetheless be the truth, or may have become the truth or even more true than truth, appeals to its public for moral endorsement to keep on going as before. All the same, it has to obscure or prune aspects of the complete context.

Palestine in its modern name and boundaries was a British manufacture. That it should be a homeland for the Jews united the Arabs of Palestine in opposition and gave them an identity they had lacked, though this in turn served to stimulate Zionist identity. The constant aim of Zionism has been to translate its will into a territorial existence, but even without such a movement the provinces of the defunct Turkish empire were vulnerable to the times. Changes in the balance of power, coupled with modern technology, were slowly crushing awkward entities everywhere, whether small states or minorities. Succeeding British governments, for all their contradictory and submerged intentions, were in this respect in the same impasse as any of their subjects. In one sense, Israel is a rearguard action against these conformist and centralizing tendencies; its stand on self-determination belongs to the age of Rousseau and Byron.

The disintegration of the European order in the thirties brought consequences which the Arabs could deplore but not dodge – one of which, and not the foremost, being a mass immigration of Jewish refugees into Palestine. The Arabs could either do their best to contain the Jews, and perhaps exploit their skills and capital, or else set their face against them. In larger terms, they were being obliged to bet on England or Germany in the coming struggle. Although some landowners were prepared to sell their estates at the prices the Jews were paying, the Palestinians hoped to hold the future in suspense until Europe had sorted itself out. The leadership was conservative-minded, and it had in Haj Amin el Hussaini, the Mufti of

Jerusalem, a spokesman who could make the most of every traditional instinct, social as well as religious. As a Hussaini, Haj Amin was a member of the most powerful clan in the country. The only rivals, the Nashashibi clan, had similar views, so that the issue between them was who should hold power. The mufti drove the Palestinians into line by every method of persuasion from bribery to terror. Fakhri Nashashibi was to claim that over the years 292 members of his faction had been murdered by the mufti's. The mufti appointed his men to an Arab Higher Committee which took upon itself authority for the Palestinians but was a means of dictating popular extremism to the masses. Irregular forces loosely called a Liberation Army were recruited and financed by the mufti and placed under the command of one of his kinsmen, Abdelkader Hussaini. A capable leader, Abdelkader Hussaini had taken to the field by the end of 1947.

Opposing nationalisms came to a trial of strength. The 1947 vote of the United Nations to partition Palestine into Jewish and Arab sectors showed that violence had as much scope under the emerging superpowers as in the days of the dying colonial empires. Israeli versions of the fighting will insist on the correctness of the Haganah, passing over with a regretful sentence the Deir Yassin massacre by the Irgun terrorists of 254 Arab villagers, pointing out that the Arabs murdered just as many civilians and brought disaster on themselves by rejecting all approaches to settlement. Arab versions insist that the Jews are all terrorists having no right to be there in the first place, and they will pass over the massacres they did on Ben Yehuda Street or on Mount Scopus with a sentence about the demands of justice. They will go on to assert that the Jews had a masterplan dating from the nineteenth century to get the land for themselves by evicting the Arabs from it.

The massacre at Deir Yassin was on 8 April, at a time when there was skirmishing across the country for control of the roads. Nearby at Castel, a few days later Abdelkader Hussaini was killed and the hopes of the irregular forces collapsed. Thousands of the more well-to-do had already sought refuge outside the country, and now in the first radiating wave of alarm a quarter of the Palestinians (or more, or less, according to sources) also anticipated the worst and fled. Such panic encouraged the remaining masses to believe that they were defenceless and about to be slaughtered in the manner of the Armenians or the Assyrians. Tiberias, Haifa, the Katamon district of Jerusalem, Safad, Jaffa – these principal centres of the Arab population were evacuated between 18 April and 13 May, and left almost entirely in the hands of the Jews. Sometimes the British army was present at these flights, and whatever it did or did not do was held responsible by either side for any misfortune. On 15 May, as the Mandate expired and the British like nervous tourists withdrew a little ahead of timetable, regular Arab armies entered Palestine from Egypt, Syria, Iraq and Transjordan.

In the years afterwards a controversy arose, as angry as it has been inconclusive: had the Arab leaders ordered the masses to flee and, if so, why, or had the Israelis expelled them? The study of the period's leaflets and press and monitored broadcasts is far from exhaustive. Such influences, and the audience accessible to them, cannot be measured. In a society like the Palestine of 1948 (or 1967) orders and appeals as well as rumours come by word of mouth quite as rapidly as on the wireless, and more effectively. Refugees in the camps today will say that they left because they were told to, on the understanding that they would be returning in the wake of the victorious Arab armies. Memory itself becomes an integral part of public opinion and realigns to keep up with it. For any rationalizations after the event, the refugees have so far stayed at the mercy of researchers whose concern in documentary material is to construct partisan briefs from it.

A local leader like Yusuf Heikal, Mayor of Jaffa, could disseminate panic, while another like Shabtai Levy, the Jewish Mayor of Haifa, could plead with Arabs not to flee. The end results were the same: whether they intended it or not, the Palestinians were accepting that their fate rested with others. Not the chief protagonists of their own war, they were the losers even before it was under way. For thirty years Palestinians of eminence had argued that they could resist the Jews only if backed by the whole Arab world. The Arab world had responded with protestations of support but more active involvement had brought little advantage and upset the powers. Now the gathering refugees were a pretext and a spur to attack: military intervention offered a chance which might never recur to make the Israelis the second losers of the war by chasing them from the land upon the heels of the Palestinians. Had that happened, would the separate Arab countries have agreed to withdraw upon a vote of thanks, leaving the mufti and his committee to head an independent Republic of Palestine? Survival in any case became a national absolute for the Israelis and they fought accordingly. In place after place Arabs and Jews staked their will and morale against each other in a people's war. Until then, it had been essential to the Israeli case that Arabs and Jews could live together, if suitably partitioned. With one truce broken and then another, this interest changed and the Israelis needed to hold territory at all costs, never mind what happened to the Arabs in it. If the Arabs who were still in the country, though reduced by earlier flights to a minority, now stayed where they were and held their peace, well and good; if they ran away without fighting, so much the better; if they were caught up in the fighting and were pushed out, so much the worse.

Historical judgements, even within their limits, have been no use to the refugees, then or since. The Armistice Agreements of 1949 found them wintering wretchedly wherever they could. The Arab countries surrounding Israel were in a quandary: they had sent off their armies to the rescue, only to bring home the Palestinian problem. Those very people for whose protection they had gone to war were now among them, but destitute, demanding more protection. Recriminations were inevitable. Once in other Arab countries, their return home blocked, the Palestinians came to see their protectors in another light, not as brothers who had done what they could but as agents in the disaster, perhaps its accomplices, even traitors to the cause. By virtue of the Partition vote, the Arab half of Palestine should have gained its independence but even that rump of the country was absorbed into the Kingdom of Jordan by King Abdullah whose Arab Legion had occupied and held it during the fighting. A military defeat as such remains unacceptable to this day; it has to have concealed depths and hidden explanations into which may be sunk the shame of not having stood against the Jews. In the years of exile that lay ahead the Palestinians have come to visualize themselves in a clamp between Israeli atrocities and Arab betrayals.

Representatives of the Palestinians arrived at various stages of the armistice talks between Israel and the Arab states – a fruitless effort to speak up for themselves when it was too late. Count Bernadotte, the mediator appointed by the United Nations, had recommended that the refugees go back home; the powers agreed, the United Nations passed a resolution to that effect in 1948 and regularly since then. The Arabs maintained that the refugees be allowed home at once, not as the subject of any bargain or peace treaty: they were extending their pre-war attitude of all-or-nothing, and they made it clear that this was a prelude to destroying Israel. The phrase 'a fifth column' was used to deadly effect by both sides. An unconditional offer by Israel in 1949 to take back 100,000 refugees was not considered sufficient. Other offers were conditional: for instance, if the Egyptians withdrew from the Gaza Strip which they continued to occupy as the spoils of war, the Israelis would take it together with a quarter of a million refugees.

Within Israel, meanwhile, Jewish immigrants were arriving in numbers almost exactly equivalent to the Palestinians who had fled, thereby creating the unbearable symmetry of one nation of refugees establishing itself on top of another. The new Israelis were also destitute, whether they were concentration camp survivors from Europe, or came from Arab countries where they were no longer safe and sometimes dispossessed. A reluctant exchange of population resulted. By a series of laws and ordinances Israel absorbed what had been Palestinian. 'Abandoned property was one of the greatest contributions towards making Israel a viable state,' is the conclusion of Don Peretz, whose book (*Israel and the Palestine Arabs*, 1958) is one of the rare pieces of sustained research on the question. Every Arab who after 29 March 1947 had left his town or village in what had become Israel was liable to be classified as an absentee, a legalism which led to hardship even for those Arabs who had stayed in the country. A Custodian of Absentee Property was appointed, and also a Development Authority which could lease land and houses owned by the refugees. The Arab nature of the country dwindled except in those places where the remaining 167,000 Palestinians lived – those who for one reason or another had not fled.

The Palestinian past survives in a fine house or street, from the days of the Turks, probably, in Jaffa or Haifa or Jerusalem. Such buildings are preserved by the richer Israelis, as though those honey-coloured stone blocks and graceful balconies promised a return to an older ease and tolerance. In the Galilee it is still possible to come upon a deserted Arab village wrapped into the hills, its walls gaping, the roofs long vanished. Not mentioned in books or documents, a place like this is its own record. On a hump, perhaps, or standing apart, is some sheikh's whitewashed tomb with its eggshell dome. Tractors drive past. The neighbouring kibbutz is likely to be farming the village's land. Neither side has been able to afford much practical pity for the other. To the Israelis, that kibbutz requires no more vindication than the annual harvest or the blue sky overhead. To the Palestinians, the ruined walls of the village provide the only history they care to remember – a nightmare of the past which is also a prophecy for the future, and a self-fulfilling one, in those tens of thousands once again in the cross between atrocity and betrayal streaming past at the bridge.

Nobody in 1948 had foreseen an Arab refugee problem, nobody expected it to be more than temporary, nobody expected the Armistice Agreements to provide boundaries which were going to have to last until another round of fighting, and then another. As is the custom, missions and commissons began to write reports and make recommendations. By the standards of the present age, this refugee problem was small and inconsequential.

In Central Europe, in India, in China, the hordes of refugees were numbered in round figures of millions and tens of millions. Bodies by a roadside were to become the universal picture of the human condition. The United Nations Economic Survey Mission for the Middle East gave the figure of 726,000 Palestinian refugees. For their purposes a refugee was defined as a person who in May 1948 had been living in Palestine for at least two years and who as a result of the 1948 war had lost his home or means of livelihood. The figure is generally accepted in spite of reservations about its computing: it was certain that some not eligible under the UN definition, but as poor or poorer than the refugees, had been able to get on the relief rolls. In 1957 the Israeli government estimated the refugees to be 'somewhere between 705,000 and 725,000'. In a study, *How Many Arab Refugees?* (1959), Dr Walter Pinner calculated that there had been originally not more than 539,000. At any rate, those who rightly or wrongly were defined as refugees came to be under the care of the United Nations, through its Relief and Welfare Agency, known by its initials as UNRWA (pronounced Un-Rah like some Nilotic god). In this respect the Arab countries may be thought to have won a diplomatic success, for no other refugees anywhere at any time have received such preferential treatment from the world community, several thousand million dollars having been spent on them up to the present. (Which goes to show, the Arabs would reply, that the world has a special standard of consideration in dealing with Israel for whom it is ready to buy a solution.)

Repatriation, resettlement, reintegration, rehabilitation: the re- words of a continuous Palestine debate. From the beginning Arab spokesmen insisted on repatriation and on nothing but that. Resettlement was at first the UNRWA policy but it depended upon the willingness of Arab countries to accept Palestinians, and that was limited by politics, finance and bias. Ambitious and expensive plans were drawn up for resettlement, plans which would have developed the overall economies of the region. Granted that the refugees were paid for by non-Arab funds, the Arab governments were not sure what to do for the best but none would be committed to anything which might prejudice the return of the Palestinians to their own country by whatever means. Emptier Arab countries like Iraq and Libya, badly in need of manpower and investment, allowed in over the years only a few token Palestinians. In the face of discouragement and rejection, UNRWA shelved its comprehensive projects and spent the money instead on routine relief. The more the Israelis listened and watched, the more determined they grew that the refugees should stay where they were. Resettlement appeared as hopeless as repatriation, which laid the Arab governments open to the accusation of exploiting the refugees for political ends, an accusation which they sometimes refuted, at other times happily admitted – the battle with Israel was to be fuelled by the frustration of the Palestinians. Was it not a battle of destiny? Palestinians might not care to fight any more if their destiny had been resettled away.

Rehabilitation had better prospects. Within a few years all refugees had been moved out of tents and into huts. Camps were erected on permanent sites. Ration rolls were organized. The UNRWA administration tactfully did whatever pleased its hosts. Syria had received some 75,000 refugees and, although it did not offer them citizenship, enabled them to take jobs and even serve in the army and bureaucracy. In the Lebanon the 100,000 refugees could not be granted citizenship because most of them were Moslems, which would tip the scales against the Christians in a country whose constitution elaborately checks and balances the one religion against the other.

Jordan, a desert emirate and the poorest of the host countries, had gained in the West Bank a potential asset, though with it came a defeated population of approximately 450,000 as well as half a million refugees who swarmed on both banks of the river. King Abdullah had always hoped to unite the Fertile Crescent countries into a Greater Syria under his rule, and here was a modest first step, one which Britain though not other countries ratified. To incorporate the West Bank and its inhabitants into Jordan was to be openly accused of betrayal and complicity with the Israelis and the British in the dismemberment of Palestine (the kind of charge which was to be heard again in 1967). King Abdullah had learnt his politics in a hard school, and in fact he was thankful that his Arab Legion had acquitted itself well and had saved the Old City of Jerusalem from the Jews. He perceived that the Israelis had got their state as a result of a history in Europe which could be abhorred by everybody but not reversed. During the Armistice Agreement talks, and for months afterwards, Israeli emissaries were invited secretly at night to the king's palace at Shuneh not far from the Allenby Bridge. Should any settlement have emerged from these talks, the king had to be able to rely on the allegiance of the Palestinians, and in this he was helped by a lucky break. The Egyptians and Haj Amin, the mufti, had been having their secret talks as a result of which in September 1948 they declared an Arab Government of All Palestine in Gaza. Haj Amin was elected president; the Arab Higher Committee sat once more. The Egyptians wanted to make sure that, in salvaging Gaza for themselves, they also deprived King Abdullah of authority over Palestinians. Few Palestinians could have confidence in such a device; Haj Amin and his Higher Committee were discredited after the defeat, to be cast aside. The many enemies of the Hussainis, and in particular the Nashashibis, took the opportunity to make a fresh tack. When King Abdullah summoned his own Palestinian Congress in Jericho and then Amman, when Palestinians were elected to the Jordanian Parliament and a Nashashibi appointed governor of the West Bank, he was surprised to discover that his new subjects might after all prove loyal.

The mufti had his revenge. In March 1951 a member of the Hussaini clan and some accomplices murdered King Abdullah as he was entering the Mosque of Omar in Jerusalem. The king was buried there in a grave not far from that of Abdelkader Hussaini, the mufti's guerrilla leader. As a name-plate on the door, the Arab Government of All Palestine in Gaza lasted until 1959 when Nasser finally discarded it, and the mufti too.

The assassination of King Abdullah gave Palestinians the feeling that obscurely an account had been settled, but it was a hindrance to getting home. The Palestinian problem had been pressed to the heart of Arab politics, where it could be a means to other Arab ends, or an end in itself, but neither peace nor war nor monarchs nor Nasser nor Ba'athists could resolve it. Palestinians in Jordan suffered from a contradiction: the more they maintained their separate identity and their rights, the more they threatened the artificial unity of the one country which had completely adopted them. If they set about liberating Palestine by force, they brought Israeli reprisals against Jordan. The Egyptians in 1955 and 1956 also fell into that trap. Sympathy for the Palestinian cause became a matter of speeches, unanimous in tone perhaps, but cautious in committal.

Deferred to, the Palestinians were on their way towards becoming a recognized feature within the wider Arab world, a minority everywhere to be sure, and discriminated against, but that is the hallmark of minorities not only in the Middle East. Their fixation with the Return could be respected as something almost sacred to them, but not calling for personal effort beyond lip-service. Reintegration might have worked. In the refugee camps the children of the first generation were themselves having children. The pressure to give way to what was called 'the refugee mentality' could be resisted. During the oil boom of the fifties, up to 200,000 Palestinians established themselves in spite of restrictions in Kuwait, Bahrain and the Gulf States. About the same number washed their hands of the business and emigrated to America, Canada and Germany.

The Palestinians in Israel had been cut off from other Arabs, but at least they had continuity, they were living where they belonged. By 1966 they were at last free from military government, they had received compensation and benefits (which they were none too sure about accepting), they had civil rights, their population had doubled. In respects which could not easily be dismissed, they were better off than their relations across the Armistice Lines in Gaza and Jordan.

Foreign parliamentarians and journalists, having adopted the Palestinians after the 1948 war, had grown impatient with them, pointing out that in Palestine they had been *fellahin* or peasants for the most part without land, that the dream of the Return was based upon false remembrance of what had been a servile past, that it was far better to make the best of it and be assimilated wherever they were – the kind of advice that like-minded people had once felt so free to give Jews. The Six-Day War, however, was a moment of assimilation of the Arabs to the Palestinians, and its effect, as improbable as a conjuror's, was to unite once more the separate pieces of Palestine. The Egyptians vanished from Gaza. King Abdullah's patient work was spirited away, practically by chance. A week after the war, and you began to wonder if the past could really be trusted at all. The Palestinians had always wanted to be within their own country and now at least half of them were, with the Israelis though, as if one of the ancient bi-national plans of high-minded Mandate personalities had come to life, and there had never been partition.

2 · The Wilderness of Sin

A captured tank had been placed on display in the forecourt of the Fredric Mann Auditorium. Its gun-barrel was smooth and thin, Russian. Already people on their way to work were pausing to stare at the Arab markings on the armour-plating, sightseers in the concrete-and-wash dawn of what promised to be another sultry Tel Aviv day. I had carried a sleeping-bag and a cardboard box full of tins, and was sweating. The other bundles lying about on the pavement not far from the tank looked stronger, more professionally tied for the expedition. We travellers eyed each other. The sun grew hotter out of the pale and humid sky. The lorries were late in picking us up. From a stall across the square I bought a sandwich, dry in its cellophane.

When Rafi arrived, he accelerated the landrover past the tank right up to the plate-glass and posters of the concert-hall. He jumped down, at a glance taking us all in. Methodically, a British army truck pulled up behind him: Desert Rat vintage, a rust-red rattle. It had broken down on the way from Jerusalem. Uri, its driver, a thickset man with a black beard, began an argument about repairs. In a single lithe move Rafi swung himself down on the ground under the front axle. The lower half of his body stuck out, long legs in khaki fatigues and boots wriggling him farther under the chassis. As he tinkered, he could be heard asking for tools. When he stood up again he rubbed his greasy hands on his trousers. The achievement was too easy, the expression on his face seemed to say.

At Rafi's orders the lorry was loaded, the sleeping-bags and food fitting into available spaces like pieces of a mosaic. We lined

up for the benches in the back – Rafi's grandfather, a couple
from Switzerland who introduced themselves as Arieh and
Carola, both rolling the 'r' in their names, the Hungarian
manager of a plant making bakery equipment, another small
and fussy man who wanted to make friends with everyone as
fast as possible by giving out his special information about the
sun-cream necessary in Sinai and the indispensable goggles
against glare. There were two or three quiet passengers whom
Rafi was later to call the *nudnikim*, or those not with it. Rafi
had been up since four o'clock. The wet stains on his army shirt
were neat and round. He ran his fingers through his hair which
was curly and blond but discoloured, almost bleached by the
sunshine. Then he started up the landrover and drove off with
one hand on the wheel, his other arm spread along the front
seat. Sometimes he would turn to watch us with the quickness
of a man doing two things at once.

The road southwards is flanked by eucalyptus trees, their
scent carrying warmer than the petrol and diesel fumes.
At Yad Mordecai we stopped to pick up five kibbutzniks
waiting in the shade, squatting under a tree. More stores of food
had to be stowed in the landrover's trailer, along with the jerry-
cans of fuel and water. Rafi had taken a submachine-gun and
some rounds of ammunition and pushed them down on the floor.
A loaded rifle was wedged into a spring-clip against the pas-
senger seat of the lorry.

The small and fussy man was busy rubbing lotion on the
bridge of his nose. He nodded at the guns. 'Marauders all over
Sinai – you've got to chase them off.' There was another stop
for a midday Tempo, the last iced drink before the desert. In
spite of its fizz Rafi drank a bottle straight down, then started
chewing on a matchstick, fraying its end into tiny spokes. He
hoped to give up smoking. His sunglasses were yellow-tinted.
The Hungarian manager of the bakery plant was telling us about
a job he had been consulted on in Nablus. 'No fire-bricks at all,'
he said, 'the whole town might have been burnt to the ground,
and the owner of the place answers that they've never had any
trouble of that kind.'

At the entrance to the Gaza Strip we wave and shout at a road-side military policeman. 'Ideal place for an ambush,' said the man next to me, leaning out of the lorry to stare at the thick cactus which lines both sides of the road. 'The Seven-Up Bottling Company of Gaza, Palestine.' A large warehouse, its planks coming apart. 'The Palestine Citrus Fruit Company.' The first time I had come to Gaza City, a day or two after the June War, a sniper had suddenly fired on the main square. At the crack of bullets the crowds had disappeared. A half-track swung out of an alley and its machine-gun opened up at the roofs. I ran to hide behind the tombstones of the central cemetery. Scores of Arab women were already lying there. They drew their veils or shawls over their face and went on talking.

'We got on very well,' said the Hungarian, 'but they wouldn't understand that it takes money to modernize. You don't call in a heating engineer just to give him cups of coffee. One day one of their boilers will burst and kill them all.'

Boys were now out begging, stretching their hands up at the trucks. Brightly coloured pots were everywhere for sale. This time a certain distance from the scene sets in: 'Fly United Arab Airlines.' The jets have been hand-painted on the hoardings and look like toys. Damascus, Rome, the Congo, Warsaw, capitals out of Gaza City as it slips already into the shapes of the imagination, beyond Rafi's curly head and his soggy match-end, beyond the scout-car patrols and troops in bushwhacker hats.

Check-points. Policemen loll about in vests, their transistors alive on their wrists with Arab music. The Gaza Strip frontier has remained where the Egyptians established it, a blue and white border pole pointing upwards. The road lengthens through dunes planted out here and there with orchards. A ditch, the railway track, and beyond it is the corner of that dead soldier with his upraised legs. I am ready to flinch again. The tyres whine and hum on the warm asphalt. In a last cultivated patch some men and women in the distance are picking grapes, while others are resting under an awning of sacks and fronds. Sitting.

In November, after five months at it, work parties were still hauling unused equipment out of the many Egyptian positions and loading it on to freight trains at El Arish. At the station siding we stopped to talk to the soldiers doing this job. The officer in charge had taken the same commando course as Rafi. In front of the camp and the aerodrome with its huts reserved for UN Yugoslavs and Canadians – their squadron numbers up on blue boards – still stands a cinderblock obelisk of Winged Victory, a monument to the Egyptian air-force. It is the one public monument in the whole desert, for its only rival, Parker's Point, set up years ago on a Sinai plateau by a British colonel with a passion for trigonometry, was destroyed after the Suez campaign as a relic of imperialism.

At El Arish the palm-trees rise in a big plantation and the town's inhabitants pass the time of day there out of the heat, with a view of the close unmoving sea. For each man and woman there must be hundreds, perhaps thousands of rounds of ammunition of all calibre now working down into the sand. Empty cases or live shells, small arms and long-range field guns, Czech, American, British, Swiss, Russian, old and new, sometimes the gift of Ministries of Defence, sometimes smuggled on black markets. People come and go. There are no souvenirs.

The hills here look as if they will rise into mountains but they never do; the plain never ends. At Bir Hassneh the trucks halted. Women to the right, men to the left. These barracks, such as they were, flimsy prefabs, have been smashed. Filing cabinets have spilled out, the forms of Egyptian bureaucracy are spreading over the sandy floors, the paper curling at the edges in the sun. We look at the junk as if we were in a second Valley of the Kings. We wipe ourselves on pages torn from a quartermaster's store issue book. Double entries, even out here. 'You should be more careful,' says the small fussy man, 'you can't tell where they might plant bombs.' Flies, immediately settling, are the only living creatures to be seen in the wilderness.

The Israelis had a big supply depot at Jebel Heifan, approaching the Mitla Pass. Our truck and landrover drew up a few hundred yards off, mere civilians. The sky has softened. The sun is bowing out fast, the light sliding to orange and even green on the horizon. A camp is set up. We all talk at once, and busybody about with tin-openers and dixies. Arieh and Carola have a range of Swiss gadgets made of chromium and aluminium. The sudden dark and even more abrupt cold of the night throw them out. The kibbutzniks on the other hand have special smocks and stocking caps and crouch over a portable stove – its flicker gives the women a rough partisan look which perhaps they would like to cultivate. Alone among us, they refuse to share food, defending principle. When things are collectively owned, there can be no guilt in being possessive about them.

I climb into my sleeping-bag. Under the stars. The generator for the army tents bangs irregularly. It catches fire and the soldiers are briefly outlined in its glare as they stand in a chain passing buckets. Their shouting and laughter come clear across the waste between them and us. When the blaze dies down, the generator continues to churn. A dog barks and will bark on two notes, high and low, all night long. It has strayed from the Bedouin, says the small fussy man who has already prepared his shaving kit for the morning. There are flints under the sleeping-bag. I lie writing notes by torchlight and I am cold under the stars of Sinai. In an encampment with a wide sight of the heavens, but cold.

'Ar-i-eh.'

'Ca-ro-la, *boker tov*.' Even at dawn they have the habits of doves.

The night is fresh on my face. Dew has fallen. The first hour of the day, the hour of mess-tins, is chill before the desert unfolds to the sun. We have been situated by Rafi in a staggering saucer of hard-baked sand; on its rim, the army. We load up. Along the road ahead, the wreckage marks the way into the Mitla. Telephone poles lurch off in a line. The roar of our engine breaks the overwhelming silence. We are thrown backwards and forwards by the potholes. We are in an unending scrapyard, in the litter of defeat where caterpillar tracks and penicillin bottles and cottonwool and mattresses and crockery lie in layers, the plucked stuffing of an army. Pyjamas, gasmasks. We all seem to feel the urge to stare at every detail. A machine-gun mounted on a troop-carrier points to the sky and someone has stuck a skull on the end of the barrel.

'Vanity of vanities,' I say aloud.

It is the Hungarian manager of the bakery plant who answers, 'And who are you to preach?' The desert fathers must have had such exchanges. Tanks have climbed like ugly mates one on top of another. Windscreens are shattered, seats ripped to the springs, bonnets are mostly up, yellow jaws that will not snap. Each vehicle has on it '*Autozavod*' in Russian letters. Camera shutters click as if over the remains of something great which has already lain in ruins for irretrievable centuries. A whole civilization lies here and will stay until at last it will become a riddle.

Rafi and Uri have turned the two trucks round, to take us on the road to the south, past Ras Jundi. In the distance ahead a small boulder lies on the tracks we are following. It proves to be another skull, and the rusty old truck, its whole frame jolting, passes over it. Rafi has been chewing another matchstick. He is the only one among us to go bareheaded – his grandfather tells him not to be such a damn fool. Retired now, the old man was a doctor, formerly from Leipzig, and tough. His daughter, also escaping from Germany, had settled on a kibbutz, burying her past in Marxism, and she had educated her son in the glow of party and proletarian solidarity. One generation – and Rafi does not understand the nuances of his grandfather's *bitte schön*.

Somehow Rafi had taken a wrong turn. An Egyptian three-tonner stood abandoned in the sand ahead and a mile or two farther off was a jeep, tyres flat and radiator drained. A wooden office chair had been set up in the emptiness, a surrealist touch, but one which brought on an exact sense of the calamity which must have happened here.

High above us flew a pair of jets, scratches in the blue.

'*Miragim!*'

Most of us waved. Had anybody sat on the chair before us, and seen Mirages overhead and gone running off nowhere? An argument about our position was ended with compasses and map-readings.

An officer in a commando unit, Rafi had been given special duties during the fighting. He shrugged, he had not even mentioned to his grandfather what he had done. But he wanted to talk. He asked me, 'Do you know Cannes? Monte Carlo?'

I said that I did.

'Have you played in the casino?'

I had not. Rafi explained that he was looking forward to the day when he would wear a 'smoking' with a rolled velvet collar and a slim bow tie. He would have thousands of dollars and the Greek shipowners would nudge each other and ask who he was.

It was midday and the landscape wrinkled with heat. Egyptian helmets studded the path like upturned mushrooms. The question of the discarded boots had been discussed all the way – pairs had been left side by side in the most forlorn places. Skeletons were more frequent now, pitched forward with legs bent under them. Long white tibias and femurs jutting through rags, the feet already gone.

From the back of the lorry came a shout. The boys wanted to stop for photographs. They piled out. Uri protested.

'Like big-game hunters.' Rafi stared moodily at his half-inch of matchstick. 'They are crazy, they want to show how strong they are.'

Arieh had a moving camera, a new Swiss model which he explained to those who took an interest in photography. The journey has made us sensitive to the flesh. We have been bruised in that boneshaker of a lorry. Sweat pours off us. The plastic water-bottles have been filled with lemonade and their necks are sticky as they are passed round. We also want to get the measure of what has happened. Those who took photographs are ashamed; those who took no photographs are also ashamed. All have their secrets, their fears. I look at the Hungarian, the retired German doctor, the kibbutzniks, one of whom is of Egyptian origins and is given to lecturing us on the Arab mind, often rather brilliantly. Uri's mother is from Iraq, his father from Poland, in fact the Warsaw ghetto.

'I ask about Monte Carlo,' Rafi was saying. He had told Uri to drive his grandfather in the landrover. I sat beside him in the front of the truck. The rubber pad on which its engine-block was mounted had perished. The gears seemed to leap out of the floor, jolting the upright rifle next to me. 'I have read this fantastic book. About a young man who was so good-looking that women would pay him. You understand? What is that called?'

I said, 'A gigolo.'

'I think it is rather a famous book but I forget the author.'

'Somerset Maugham?'

'I am telling you, David, I should like to live in Monte Carlo. Rich women would telephone – Rafi, we can't live without you for another five minutes. Women with perfume and silk clothes. Some of the girls who visit our kibbutz are quite shameless. You wouldn't believe what they will do so that back home they can say they have had a real Israeli boyfriend. It isn't a man they want. They are like our crazy big-game hunters, they want to see themselves in poses with Jewish sufferers and heroes. You think I could become a gigolo?'

I saw the thin golden hairs on his wiry brown fore-arms. Engine-oil had worked into the skin of his fingers. His army clothes, worn and unwashed as they were, looked tight-fitting. An athlete's body – and the rich women would never know what they owed to the Hashomer Hatzair Youth Movement which went on teaching the class struggle and proving that all men are brothers.

The scenery was changing. We passed through a narrow gorge. It had been mined and the route was torn apart where the Egyptians had blown themselves up as they fled. Bits of their equipment had been flung high off the road. Danger signs and warning tapes had been strung on all sides. A few defences were visible, thin piles of stones. The sand, mixed at last with earth, had become brown.

'I respect a cultured life,' Rafi said, 'the kind of life our kibbutz cannot give us. Very good people, of course, but they have cut themselves off. They worry very much about me and my ideas. They know Marx and Lenin by heart but they do not know human beings. So I am leaving.' He put another matchstick between his teeth and started to nibble at it. 'I will tell you my idea for a big fortune, David, and if you like you will be my partner.' He turned for a moment to look at the passengers at the back. 'Before the fighting there used to be many prostitutes for the Arabs on the West Bank. You know how the Arab women are not allowed to mix with the men in society. These girls had been fetched from Germany and they made a fantastic business. When we came, these German girls could not stand the sight of so many Jews, so they have all run away. The Arabs are very frustrated. We can provide better than German girls for them, we can provide Jewish girls. If they have Jewish girls to love they will fulfil their hatred for us. And then we make enough money for Monte Carlo. And the Arabs will make peace.'

He laughed. 'What else are we to do?' The matchstick was being pulped. He spat out a sliver of wood. Then, in a different voice, 'In a few kilometres, I am telling you, there is something disgusting.'

The road levelled, the truck no longer juddered so violently. At the top of a long rise came a view of the distant sea, a mauve layer beyond the burnt and shimmering flats. And there, at the place where they too must have seen the sea and the faraway glinting storage tanks of Ras Sudr, lay the skeletons, soldiers for whom this sight of salvation after their flight had been too much. Like the others on that trail they lay as they had fallen, past endurance, but together.

When we reached Ras Sudr, where the water running in a channelled trench was poisonous with chemical waste, we pulled up and opened some tins of pineapple. The Suez shore is bleak. Close to, the sea – below the Bitter Lakes – is hardly blue, it has a grey glitter.

'Tonight we sleep at Abu Rodeis,' Rafi was explaining, 'the army will give us a special place.'

Abu Rodeis is a forlorn coastal oil-town, a scatter of huts splintering in the climate. On one cement wall in the barracks the Egyptians have left a cartoon of a mouse-like figure with an eye-patch squeaking under the heel of a black boot. The Israeli soldiers were behaving like Texas cowboys. Their commanding officer was known as Doublejack, a man with an open shirt displaying a hairy chest. He seemed to like staying up all night, shouting, and revving around in his command car.

The final seven-hour ascent to St Catherine's monastery began the following morning with a drive along wadis, passing now and then a tamarisk or some scrub. Here in the south rise chain upon chain of granite mountains, reddish brown, serrated into fantastic ranges. No wonder God was supposed to have made himself known on Mount Sinai, for this landscape is a mockery of man : 'that great and terrible wilderness,' Lawrence of Arabia called it. At the beautiful primitive oasis of Feiran, Bedouin children come running under the palm-trees begging not for cigarettes but for aspirins to cure colds. In a cleft between towering rocks the monastery at last appears, sheltered by cypresses. Its fortified walls have been much repaired but it is a survival of Byzantium, out of its time and place. Behind the church is a corner with a charming little climbing briar like a blackberry. It is protected by a blue paling and has a label on a small board: *The Burning Bush*.

The abbot, Father Nicoandros, is well over seventy, and so are Fathers Eusebius and Jeremias who have only to light or snuff the candles in church. Father Eusebius grows tomatoes and basil and talks of fighting the Turks long ago. Catering is done by Father Anastasios, a young man from Alexandria. Seven monks and a novice have fifteen Bedouin servants and cooks. Rafi and all of them were off to Sharm el-Sheikh and I decided to hitch-hike later with one of the army vehicles which call at the monastery. In the afternoon, then, we roared off past the steward on his donkey jogging to the monastery quince and almond-trees at Rabah. It seemed only proper justice that the army trucks should run out of petrol. We waited without food and water in that vast pit of stony silence under the blinding clarity of the Sinai light. It was an intimation of fate, until Bedouin eventually appeared and gave the Israelis the petrol they needed.

Back at Abu Rodeis I tag along with the soldiers. Nobody mentions passwords as I wander in and out of these dirt-blown barracks. I enter a likely-looking office and find its walls covered in production charts and technical tables of one sort or another. The Italian State oil company (with a Vatican minority holding) has the concession here but works with whoever is in control. Some manager walks in and is scandalized to find me staring at his charts. He insists on going to Doublejack. Alerts are sounded – I hear my name broadcast on the camp loud-speaker – sentries scurry. Doublejack is puzzled and sends for an intelligence officer who asks me the same questions until it is dusk and I have lost my temper. Which also makes me under-stand how expert an interrogator this man is and how quickly and ignorantly I should spill the beans if I ever had any. At dawn a plane is flying soldiers home and Doublejack chucks one of them off in order to get rid of me. So suddenly deprived of leave, this poor man is left yelling about injustice.

Four years have passed and the props are beginning to look like fixtures. That winter after the war, they had been improvising the Bar-Lev line along the Suez Canal out of the old railway tracks and sleepers and whatever else was handy. Since then, massive artillery barrages have been laid down on it, a war of attrition has come and gone, the United Nations special envoy and the American Secretary of State have come and gone, Russian missiles have come and not gone, Nasser has died. Oil production in Sinai is four times what it used to be. The manager who had me arrested by Doublejack has himself been arrested in a scandal which makes Abu Rodeis a small-scale Las Vegas. Truce or no truce, St Catherine's is on the tourist circuit – This Land Is Yours With Egged Tours, as the advertisers will have it – and I go back there in a six-seater Cherokee operated in a shuttle by a commercial company. Father Nicoandros sleeps a lot of the time now and receives nobody. Father Anastasios slipped somewhere on the mountains and was killed. The Cherokee hops on to Sharm el-Sheikh, putting down on the new landing-strip which has arrester-gear for Phantoms. Some Mirages are aligned suspiciously like dummies (living up to their name, in some air-force joke). To be precise, these barren flats are Ophir – 'Quinquireme of Nineveh from distant Ophir,

Rowing home to haven in sunny Palestine. . .'. A short coach-ride away are the gayest of tents and a dining-hall of an inflatable plastic rather like a stranded barrage balloon. The sea is tepid. Lots of visitors are expected in off-season months, to admire the tiger fish and the spiked Egyptian guns. Airborne again, the Cherokee flies along the Straits of Tiran with a view of a burnished Saudi Arabian coastline. The Sinai mountains glare up as insurmountable as the very obstacles to peace. Strategic considerations versus human needs: it is here, in this eternal wilderness, that the Palestine problem lies improbably balanced, before it can begin to wind towards an ending – as tortuously as the new road silvery and thin below the Cherokee bumping up from Sharm.

3 · *The Battle of Karameh*

The button bombs which the small fussy man had worried about in the desert were the scare of that autumn. Photographs of these miniaturized devices, which were billed as Chinese-made, had appeared in the papers. The Palestine resistance movement was in operation and anything, it seemed, might explode in one's face. The sight of an irregular parcel or of an uncollected dust-bin produced some officiousness on the part of the retired reservists who had been mobilized as watchmen. In a Home Guard spirit they patrolled the streets in pairs. What had been called the honeymoon period after the war, in which Arabs and Israelis had been so unexpectedly thrown at one another, was over.

The first to suffer were the new refugees across the river. The deadline for their return had been extended by the Israelis to the end of August, then of September, but only 14,056 officially came back, or less than half the quota. Whether the repatriation forms should have been printed in Arabic only, or in Hebrew as well, had given rise to the usual polemics. In the first week of August demonstrations and strikes were planned, and on the 8th the Jordanian finance minister, Abdel Wahab Majali, made an appeal to West Bankers now in Amman: 'Every refugee should return to help his brothers to continue their political action and remain a thorn in the flesh of the aggressor until the crisis has been solved.' The Israelis were lucky to have such a quotation handed to them. Nor were the refugees eager to go back on such terms for they had escaped in the first place in order not to be thorns in anyone's flesh. The Jordanian government naturally

37

could not accept the recent annexation of Jerusalem and it encouraged resistance. Funds were channelled over from Amman to subsidize officials, teachers and lawyers who refused to return to their jobs. Those willing to work were labelled as collaborators in leaflets printed in Jerusalem, and they were threatened with execution. The Jordanian prime minister, Sa'ad Jumaa, declared that cooperation with Israel would be regarded as treason 'to be punished in due course'.

As early as 22 June Assifa, the military wing of Fatah, largest of the Palestinian armed organizations, had announced the transfer of its headquarters to occupied territory. Hundreds of guerrillas, idealists, militants, students, bracketed together generically as *fedayeen* (literally meaning those who are ready to sacrifice themselves for the cause), and recruited among Palestinians everywhere in the world, were rumoured to be converging on the West Bank and forming underground cells. Under the military government of a few weeks' standing, the Israeli security police had to deal with this development, and it was helped to a flying start by having inherited full intelligence files from the previous Jordanian military government. Those who had been agitating against King Hussein's rule were switching to take on Israel, but without the protection of secrecy.

Theoretically, or according to the doctrines of Mao Tse-tung and Ho Chi Minh, the *fedayeen* had the advantage, swimming as they were supposed to among the population like fish in water. Palestinians were disposed to see the liberation movement as their one hope of freeing themselves from atrocity and betrayal, from Israelis and Jordanians. Probably the need for such a hope (as well as the urgency of beating the Amman government to the draw) impelled the *fedayeen* into acts of sabotage which were limited in scope through lack of planning. On 25 August the campaign opened on the West Bank when a young man fired on Israeli cars from Abu Dis on the Bethlehem road. As a punishment, five houses in which he and his accomplices had sheltered in the village were dynamited. On the face of it Arabs and Israelis were reverting to the late 1947 vicious circle of incident and reprisal. In direct consequence the refugees on the East Bank ceased to exert further pressure to return home. They preferred to stay out of harm's way. Quotas and deadlines became irrelevant.

On 19 September another general strike was declared throughout the West Bank to coincide with the opening of the General Assembly of the UN. Nablus, where half the schools were refusing to open for the academic year, was the only town to observe the strike. Six days later the Israeli security forces closed in with tanks on what turned out to be the Fatah, or Assifa, headquarters in the *casbah* of Nablus. Only one guerrilla was killed and one taken prisoner although a few hours later several more were arrested after a search and chase by helicopter. The inference was made: the Nabulsis had gone on strike because the Fatah was generally known to be active among them. Conversely, then, if the Fatah were absent, the population might stay passive. The failure of the general strike outside Nablus suggested that the Israelis would be able to drive a wedge between the *fedayeen* and the ordinary people. This might be done all the more efficiently because the *fedayeen* had drawn attention to themselves so prematurely, before allowing time to consolidate.

The *fedayeen* seemed to have sensed as much, for in the subsequent months their tactics were directed at arousing Israeli retaliations. Military targets were ignored. Bombs were placed in cinemas or garages or the American Embassy library, partly because this was not very risky to do but also because outrages against civilians might provoke infuriated mobs of Jews to rush out on to the streets and kill innocent Arabs. Coexistence would then be out of the question; rioting and loss of life would make Arabs and Israelis uncontrollable, and the burden of occupying the West Bank would be so intolerable that the Israelis would withdraw. Possibly the *fedayeen* organizations suspected that in their mood of postwar demoralization the West Bankers could not be counted on for heroics, though the Israelis might still be tempted into making the oldest of colonial mistakes, which is to use force so indiscriminately and ruthlessly that moderates are converted into extremists.

To woo ordinary people away from the resistance movement the Israeli administration gave them every inducement to go about their business as before, and to sit tight pending a political settlement. Government was limited, the military presence concealed. Israel's good fortune was to be able to profit from Jordan's misfortune. The East Bank needed the agricultural supplies of the West Bank and anyhow could not abandon territory over which it claimed sovereignty. The Allenby and Damia bridges have continuously remained open, facilitating from the beginning what has been almost normal peacetime life for those who want to lead it. With a permit to buy and sell or to visit their relations, they may come and go as they please on either side of the river and thus are not isolated in tension under Israeli rule. The Jordanians have had no choice but to undermine the resistance they promote.

Whatever guerrilla doctrine might preach, the West Bank is not Vietnam. The mountains of Judaea and Samaria, though wildly beautiful, are empty and stony. Movement is easy to spot and to control. Crossing the river Jordan, infiltrators have to climb out of the deep valley, to labour up rocky slopes carrying any arms and equipment. Then they had to be able to rely on West Bankers (who might after all be their families and friends) for food, shelter and disguise. Some of the first groups, for example, used to make for Jiftlik, the only village below the plateau – with the inevitable result that in November the Israeli army evacuated the adobe houses there. Such punishments were swift and drastic enough to be a deterrent. Anybody who helped the *fedayeen* might be arrested, sentenced to prison, and have his house demolished under Emergency Regulations drawn up by the British and applied wholesale during a crisis like the Arab revolt of 1936. Demolition of houses could be arbitrary in that the owner might well not be responsible for the arrival of the *fedayeen* there – he might have let the house, or be away or have emigrated to America – but still he had to bear the loss. The local population at once perceived that it was going to suffer from *fedayeen* activity at least as much as the Israelis did, if not more. Sympathetic as they might be to the cause, they had little to gain in the short run and much to lose – and the long run could take care of itself. Guerrilla success could be bought only at their expense. A lot of trouble was saved by giving the Israeli security forces a quiet tip-off.

In the last three months of 1967 networks of *fedayeen* were captured complete, twenty and thirty men at a time, in Jenin and Hebron and Jerusalem and Ramallah. One group was led by Mustafa Khamis from a prominent Hebron family. Faisal Hussaini, the son of Abdelkader Hussaini of 1948 fame, was arrested after only a few days on the West Bank, and so was Taysir Kubbeh, president of the General Union of Palestinian Students. Touad Abdul Hadi, from an old Nablus family and well-known as the headmistress of a girls' school, was also arrested. As the Popular Front for the Liberation of Palestine, the PFLP for short, set itself up in some competition to the Fatah, its main organizers on the West Bank, including Ahmed Khalifa and his contact Khalil Touami, were rounded up. If the story is to be believed, Yasser Arafat himself, the head of the Fatah, escaped out of the back window of a house in Ramallah while the police were bursting in at the front. The *fedayeen* were pushed out of towns and villages, then out of caves and hiding-places, and finally, by about February 1968, off the West Bank altogether.

Immediately they took up positions just across the river on the East Bank, from where they could infiltrate back. The pre-war situation had been restored, though with this difference that now any guerrilla attack brought down Israeli reprisals not on the West Bank but on Jordan proper. As the guerrillas established their new ground along the river they intensified declarations of war. With the heedless impatience which had defused their sabotage on the West Bank, they began bazooka shelling into Israel. No sooner did Israeli aircraft in turn bomb *fedayeen* outposts than the inhabitants of the Jordan valley fled away up the mountains behind them. Another exodus, another escape from a battlefield. About 100,000 people or more were displaced. Some of them were peasant farmers, some of them refugees who had either been settled in camps in the valley like Karameh, or who had been under temporary cover since the previous June (in holiday tents, as it happened, from America, and all in seaside colours). A good proportion of the latter were on the run for the third time since 1948. In this flight were several implications for the future, but one clear present conclusion: that *fedayeen* action resulted in moving the refugees not westwards home but eastwards towards the desert.

In the middle of February King Hussein said in a speech that he would not permit anyone to provide the enemy of his homeland with more excuses to inflict more harm than the enemy had already done. At the same time he declared that he could not make himself responsible for Israel's security by restraining the *fedayeen*. The dilemma was not to be resolved until the civil war two years later. Jordan had wished the Palestinian resistance on to Israel, and the compliment had been returned.

The proverbial sticks and carrots were being proferred to the West Bankers in this three-cornered contest over their heads between the *fedayeen*, the Jordanians and the Israelis. But how to distinguish them, and which to accept? Whose claims were likeliest? Morale swung up and down. After the war everyone had their proposals for a settlement. Among the most clear-minded was Dr Kadri Tuqan, a former Jordanian cabinet minister and one of the best-known intellectuals in the Arab world. He lived in Nablus. To meet him at that time was to catch up on current ideas, on the straws in the wind. He had a twinkle in his eye and liked to show off his signed photographs of Nasser or of his reception into the Egyptian Academy of Sciences. A few months later even someone so independent had become broodier. In Ramallah Dr Hamdi Faruki who had been presenting the Palestinian case as far back as 1948 and was now advocating some arrangement with the Israelis had had his windows blown in by a bazooka shell. The Mayor of Ramallah, Nadim Zahrou, was shot at by the Fatah and later deported by the Israelis – an unhappy example of playing the two ends off against the middle. Nobody dared do more than wait and see.

Under the strain of uncertainty, the West Bank as a whole went into a period of suspended animation.

Israeli spokesmen and soldiers, including General Uzi Narkiss, the Military Governor of the West Bank, were claiming at the time to have won a conclusive victory by having driven the *fedayeen* right out of Palestine. In spite of his job, General Narkiss was accessible, informal. In his house at Zahala, where the senior Israeli commanders live, some photographs of the war show him striding along but outflanked between his taller neighbours, Generals Dayan and Bar-Lev. He was one of the first Israelis whom I had heard speaking about the *fedayeen* as if they were good boys gone astray, in tones of cool-headed regret which many others later adopted. For every guerrilla captured in action, the general said, forty were rounded up through denunciation. Nothing could be kept secret in a society crisscrossed with family or clan allegiances and enmities which kept everyone on the watch. Some of the tip-offs were simply to settle an old feud, or to start a new one, or for the sake of earning a few pounds. The week before, the Israeli security forces had planted an informer in a village to contact some known guerrillas. Within twenty-four hours the man had been denounced by his own brother, blown for getting on with the job, as it were.

Adnan Mansour, a Palestinian officer attached to the Iraqi army, had been denounced on his mission against Israel by the PFLP as a reprisal against another denunciation of PFLP men by the Fatah. The two factions were like the Hussainis and the Nashashibis all over again. The general explained how hoods were put over *fedayeen* prisoners and informers to prevent their identification, and how they then drove round in jeeps with the security forces picking out colleagues for arrest. Intelligence officers were swamped with information, they had too complete a picture. The demolition of houses, however, had to continue, it was in the best interest of the West Bankers because it gave them a real reason for refusing to help the guerrillas – Mrs Narkiss disagreed, and not for the first time, evidently, pleading with her husband as in a classical drama to change his mind. The *fedayeen* were posing a problem not to the Israelis but to the Jordanians, who could not decide how far to cooperate. The general would arrange that we go together on an ambush down by the river and I would see for myself the Jordanian army standing by 'like United Nations observers' if the *fedayeen* and the Israelis exchanged fire. Out came his notebook, and we agreed upon Thursday, 21 March at six in the morning.

At sunset on the Wednesday evening the streets of Jerusalem shook with a convoy of about thirty tank transporters and their supply trucks, followed by soldiers in buses. In the city silent Arabs gathered to watch them go through to Jericho. The Israelis usually mount their military operations behind a screen of security and this rumbling hour-long procession was as good as a telephone call to the Jordanians to tell them what to expect. Next morning I was woken up by jets whining in the thin air of the Jerusalem dawn. On my hotel balcony I could glimpse them vanishing beyond the Dead Sea, already over the East Bank. The sun began to infuse the walls of the Old City. Exactly on the hour, the telephone rang and the secretary told me what I had guessed already, that the general was unexpectedly detained and could not come with me to the river. The Israelis had crossed over to attack the *fedayeen* bases at Karameh on the East Bank.

Later it was possible to follow the road to a point east of Jericho, below the monastery of Karantel, from where the fighting on the East Bank was visible. Soft plumes of black smoke rose from the mountainside and in the valley around Karameh the tanks swirled up dust. An Israeli staff officer came to give an incoherent briefing. Helicopters flew back and forth, ferrying informers and prisoners. Around midday the booms ahead ceased.

Next day I was due to cross to Amman. The Governor of Jericho, a laconic major, turned everybody back. He and his men sat in the front garden of their headquarters, a stately villa with climbing bougainvillea, and sipped soda. On the Sunday a would-be rabbi from Chicago, now a press officer clumsy in his conscript's uniform, escorted me down to the bridge. A mild spring sun on the oleanders and willows. The bridge had been restored with an improvised pontoon, the queues of Arabs were again busy in the sheds of bureaucracy behind and ahead – and in the middle, with my awkward suitcase, I hesitated. Only nine months ago the refugees had passed. To cross is somehow to make a commitment where none is intended. Changing currency, changing gossip, changing perspective, all by setting foot on these wooden wobbly planks, the most artificial of demarcations – when the only wish is to have friends on both sides of this river.

Here was a white tent hotting up and stifling, and the police corporal who took my passport was wearing a colonial-style helmet with a polished spike. 'We catch someone from Israel, we shoot him,' as he said with the biggest of smiles. Six road-blocks to pass. Five carriers were hauling smashed tanks. Shuneh, where King Abdullah used to receive his night visitors from Israel, had been badly battered. Half its school was knocked down and the houses were pockmarked with small-arms fire. One or two dead animals lay stiff in the fields. Troops were everywhere on the road and in the hills, aimlessly energetic, like wasps.

The East Bank was all that the West Bank was not – anti-aircraft guns at strategic points including the Basman Palace where the king was living; blue paint daubed over cars' head-lights; DPs everywhere; a man from Bethlehem on the radio explaining that little white flags should be hung out for safety if the Israelis invaded. The Israelis had indeed set foot in Jordan, but only for a day. Even if they had come that much closer, even if they were to return again in strength, they had gone.

Down near the market in Amman is a Roman amphitheatre, a charming relic from the province of Peraea. Sometimes open-air plays are held in it. Close by is the Philadelphia Hotel, not quite what it used to be, but keeping something from the years when the officers of the Transjordan Frontier Force and the colonial police and their wives, either local or passing on to Palestine or Iraq or India, would have a snifter here, and maybe a bite of supper. Now next to it on an empty lot on Philadelphia Street three wrecked Israeli tanks, a half-track, a lorry and a jeep were being exhibited. It was a good, and in fact unique, haul. Day and night the inspecting crowds clambered over the vehicles. Even taxi-drivers would slow down to make sure that foreigners did not miss so much joy, thereby attracting faces in excitement round at the windows. No inconspicuous get-away from this. One of them made me get out to have a look. In anticipation the crowd fell back, a path was opened to bear me up to the tank. Sure enough, the tell-tale Hebrew lettering was on its gun-barrel. The tank had received a direct hit, it was scorched and flared, and there in the midst of charred metal the driver crouched with his safety-straps buckled on, immutable, incinerated crisp as a mummy – a figure of death itself at its darkest celebration. They were silent to watch for a response. They needed no convincing, they were killing hundreds of Jews every day – didn't the Fatah say so? – it was the doubting foreigner who had to complete the pageant, to acknowledge in his own person, as the living imperialist to the dead, that the Arabs were victorious. As I turned away they broke into cries more jubilant than ever.

In the annals of the Palestine liberation movement Karameh is the supreme battle honour. Many pamphlets and articles hail Karameh as the turning of the tide, when at last Palestinians confronted Israel, to begin the slow but triumphant surge homewards. The Israelis published the figure of twenty-three dead, which was high for such an operation: their press was also critical of the restrictions placed upon the army for political reasons. Palestinian militants dismissed as lies such Israeli statements, just as they minimized the role of the Jordanian army in support at Karameh. Analysis, facts, would throw shadows over the bright hour. Guerrillas, Chairman Mao had decreed, should never oppose a regular army, but here they were breaking the rules. They had put a stop to running away and had something to show for it. Between 150 and 200 *fedayeen* had been killed at Karameh; their funerals were not occasions for grief, but parades of heroism. The small sons of the dead were kitted out with flak-jackets and marched by the coffins of their fathers, to unite past and future, performance and promise. A whole people was to arise in an epic of revenge, and the humiliation suffered for so many years would be burnt out like that Israeli tank-driver. Otherwise Karameh would not have been such a victory, there would have been no obsession about it – humiliation and victory became one and the same thing in the talk of liberation, and the Republic of Palestine became the Vietcong, a New Age, Overthrowing the System (phrases, as they sounded afterwards, more akin to an American youth festival).

Offices of the Resistance proliferated, on the Jebel Hussein, the Jebel Webdeh, in Ashrafiya, round the Second Circle: Fatah, the PFLP, the PLO, other groups. The moment the Israelis had pulled back, spokesmen from these offices were sponsoring tours to Karameh. Their cars would simply ignore Jordanian army roadblocks and swerve past to a tame salute. Karameh, a rough place at any time, had been expertly dynamited. From every telephone pole along the road the lines drooped to the ground. But the commandos had returned, to be compared, one thought for a moment, to the people of Kalkilya. In the foothills they were dug into the ruins of their emplacements, they were going through the motions of fieldcraft, they were cleaning weapons with oily flannelette. They were young. The holiday atmosphere was catching. We were on an outing in the open air brewing up coffee on a kerosene stove with a palm-tree or two and banana groves in the background, and adventure all around. The Israelis were a few kilometres off, they had entered into the spirit of the thing and brought all this on themselves: it was more a chase than war. An officer casually introduced himself to say that the Israelis had merely strengthened those whom they had intended to root out. The Israelis did his recruiting for him, as we could see. Palestinian resistance, the world was to learn, was the coming force to be reckoned with; Jordan was falling apart at the seams, occupied by the Israelis on the West Bank, by a division or so of Iraqis at Zerqa, by Saudis at Ma'an. King Hussein would have to bow to popular will, and maybe abdicate.

The streets of Amman suddenly belonged to the *fedayeen*, who lorded it in twos and threes, laughing and horse-playing, or careening about in jeeps breaking traffic regulations while the police looked on and the citizens admired their new masters. In front of the main mosque lorries would pass with recruits in the back chanting 'Fatah Fatah Fatah'. They wore camouflage uniforms and webbing with ammunition pouches. They liked weapons. They went into the *souks* and demanded money from the merchants who were happy to pay, in a hurry, though afterwards lodging a complaint which stayed in somebody's file and was forgotten. They lifted dollar bills out of the wallets of foreigners with a certain elegance and a smile, because they knew that nobody would argue, not right there in the bazaar with the memorial posters to dead comrades pasted up all round.

On the East Bank, as on the West Bank, the allegiance of the population was at stake in a contest between government and *fedayeen*. No group, not even Fatah, with a few thousand members, could hope to achieve its aim of national liberation unless it grew into a mass movement. The refugees were ideal material – again according to the books – they were the victims of colonialism, imperialism, Zionism, the wretched of the earth, peasants who must rise up and free themselves. Fatah was only one among several resistance organizations who, in the competition for funds and volunteers, set up recruiting centres in the camps, hoping to tap the misery not only of twenty years but of the cold winter after the Six-Day War. The emergency camps had bad sites on windswept desert plains or in areas which had to be changed to suit the military situation. Some of the new DPs had been moved three times since June. They went from camp to camp now, and to the towns in search of a living. The actual population of Baqa'a, supposedly 44,000, might be considerably higher or lower, as the official UNRWA statement put it. The tents were flapping bundles of blackened canvas pitched in rows with the mud caking between them. The DPs were living in a whirl of disturbance and makeshift poverty, they had quite lost what had seemed the sense of purpose carrying them to the bridge in the summer. They queued for water at the standpipes, they queued for food, they sat on the earth jostling in dozens at any door which might offer something, rations or medicine or compassion.

Same sight at the Hussein camp, at Schneller, up at Irbid. The Jerash camp lies at the end of a road which twists past some olive groves into low hills, at the back of beyond. For some reason it was known as Gaza camp, and it had space reserved for future refugees. Apparently everyone expected the Israelis to be soon driving out all the West Bankers, and they could do nothing about it except have spare tents ready. The Fatah tent stood in a prominent spot, and passed for a youth centre, with perhaps a dozen teenagers in it, waiting, day after day. On a blackboard was pinned the portrait of a dead Fatah commando between crude chalk drawings of guns. A ping-pong table had been presented by some charity or other, and we played for a part of the afternoon until the enervation of the tap-tapping ball was too much. I had come with someone from the Save the Children Fund, and he was trying to track down people who claimed to have been napalmed by the Israeli air-force during the war. There were none. These refugees had not seen an aeroplane, let alone a bomb. It seemed insulting to probe into their tents for a minute or two at a stretch, and put into their minds that they had been through worse atrocities than this, what with the damp and the smells and the cowed children. Their lives were being tied to the uses of our consciences. Nobody came into the Fatah tent either; it was soon twilight, too dark to see, and time to leave.

The Ministry of Reconstruction in Amman is a fine villa, in stone. Every day since the war scores of DPs had been pressing at the entrance and clamouring to be registered for a ration card and relief. Women were suckling babies on the ministry steps. The corridors were blocked by petitioners with workworn country faces unaccustomed to this sort of mob. In an outer waiting-room were a dozen notables and beyond sat the minister, from a well-known Palestinian family. Good modern chairs of chrome and leather. He too was under the Karameh spell: six hundred Israelis were dead, he knew it for a fact, just as he had seen the charred tank-driver padlocked into his seat. It was shaming to be wasting an hour of his time in an interview, while the hum of distress reached through the open window, as it would for weeks and months to come. Any foreign correspondent gets away with it, of course; he stuffs the notes of his story into a pocket, shakes hands, and pushes through the mothers and babies, observing their skin diseases and sores. His self-importance soars. For him the government car is ordered, the guide is politely sitting in it (another graduate from America, to match the would-be rabbi on the other side), to drive with him down to the bridge, and help with the suitcases. The Jordanian police in their spiked helmets and then the Israelis will greet him as he moves among the travelling Arabs the way a corked bottle bobs on the seas. It is not his fault, any more than it is the fault of the minister, of the charred tank-driver, of the teenagers around a ping-pong table dreaming of murder, or of simple people who have no idea what hit them, or even perhaps of arms-dealing thugs in faraway capitals who know quite well. In their separate ways they confirm what they cannot change.

Refugee and guerrilla: two alternating images of himself for the Palestinian to choose. Reality blinded him with self-pity, he was poor, let-down, the object of charity and its twin contempt, too demoralized to do anything about it – but reverse the slant and he was free, taking over his destiny and, if need be, a martyr to it. Disaster into hope, black and white, refugee into guerrilla: is not this the age when opposites become one and the same? Palestinians did not escape this dialectic. Those who might prosper as doctors, contractors, teachers, bankers, were often self-made men. Feeling guilty about the masses below them, they needed more than anyone to atone by contributing time and money to the cause. During the 1950s the Palestine cause was the preserve of intellectual and professional classes. Dispersed among Arab countries, they were subordinated to Arab politics as a matter of practical organizing but also because Arab unity by common consent was the prerequisite to the recovery of Palestine. The Sinai campaign of 1956 compounded failure on this score: perhaps Arab unity would not after all precede the liberation of Palestine but be its consequence: perhaps Palestinian nationalism was not pan-Arab in spirit but quite separatist. Such abstractions properly belonged to debating circles and the pages of specialized magazines. In order to turn them into a programme, Palestinians of every hue had to find a flag of convenience under which to sail.

Some like Dr George Habash and his friend Dr Wadi Haddad belonged to the Arab Nationalist Movement, became enthusiastic supporters of Nasser, before moving leftwards in disillusion to found the PFLP. Its policy is first to liberate Palestine and then to govern it in accordance with Marxism-Leninism. Yet after Karameh it was the Soviet-backed Syrian government which put Habash and Haddad into prison, from which they were rescued in circumstances which are obscure. That the Syrian government and the PFLP are in doctrinal harness does not stop the former carefully controlling the latter on its territory. Other Palestinians like Yasser Arafat (a relation and one-time secretary of Haj Amin, the Mufti of Jerusalem) began as members of the right-wing Moslem Brotherhood, and Fatah as they founded it in the 1950s was a traditional kind of secret society. Yet as from 1965 Fatah was supported by the Syrians and clamped on by the Jordanians. Ideology, in short, was bound up with opportunity. The entire Palestine resistance movement has put down such roots as it could in the stony crevices of inter-Arab rivalry.

The idea of an independent Palestine entity was too expedient to be overlooked among the ruins of war, for depending on local factors it could embarrass Jordan, Egypt or the resistance groups themselves, indeed anyone who espoused the cause for whatever reason, even Israel. President Aref of Iraq made the running over such an entity but Nasser outflanked him. In 1964 Israel was proposing to go ahead with its share in the development of the Jordan waters. At the Arab summit conference which followed, Nasser said that Egypt for the present was not ready for war on this question – something of a scandal which he averted by setting up the Palestine Liberation Organization. Funds were to come from the Arab League. Its appointed leader was Ahmed Shukeiry, a lawyer from Jaffa, sometime spokesman for the mufti, sometime Saudi delegate to the UN and a rogue elephant in Arab politics. In Jerusalem in May 1964 Shukeiry presided over the first of a series of Palestinian National Congresses, which in turn erected a whole bureaucracy of committees and sub-committees, with presidents and treasurers. Representatives were posted in Arab countries, and in Peking. A national anthem was adopted and also a flag, identical to the Jordanian except for an additional star.

The PLO soon had an army of about 10,000 under training mostly in the Gaza Strip where they were fully under Egyptian control. Jordan could not very well refuse to have the PLO on its territory, or else its Palestinian subjects would be up in arms. Fatah, however, was quicker off the mark than the PLO and laid their first mine on a road in Israel on 1 January 1965. They had been supplied with Syrian arms and money. If the Egyptians could make capital out of the Palestine problem, as the politics of the moment suggested, then so could their former allies but present rivals, the Syrians. On condition, however, that Fatah did not operate out of Syria but first entered Jordan and started raids from there against Israel. With similar precaution the PLO was restricted to internal subversion and propaganda. In their separate ways Egypt and Syria had backed Palestinian resistance in a manner calculated to bypass the consequences.

Israeli reprisals would no doubt be lethal but would fall on Jordan where Fatah ostensibly began its operations, and one such reprisal of great severity in November 1966 on the West Bank village of Samu did almost split open the Hashemite Kingdom. The West Bankers requested weapons to defend themselves and help the *fedayeen*. PLO agents agitated in the camps, whipping up the refugees to fight the Israelis and the Jordanians. Shukeiry himself was credited with the slogan of the hour, 'To liberate Tel Aviv we must first liberate Amman.' Riots in the towns of the West Bank had to be suppressed by the army in a state of emergency.

A Palestinian entity or independence of any kind or shape could only be at Jordan's expense. Jordanian interests were not Palestinian but the contrast had never been so blatant or danger-

ous. The government moved against the Fatah, and closed down
the PLO offices in Amman. From Cairo Shukeiry campaigned
against what he called the 'dwarf-king' until the very eve of the
Six-Day War. Then King Hussein flew to Cairo to mend his feud
with Nasser and took Shukeiry on board his own aircraft for
the return flight to Amman. Shortly afterwards the king's fears,
and the Palestinian resistance movement's hopes, were both
realized, although not as they had anticipated. And Israel picked
up the pieces of the quarrel.

After the war the PLO was in disarray, its army either mauled
or melted away into the civilians of Gaza which they really
were. Shukeiry was disgraced and in December 1967 he was
replaced by Yahya Hammoudia, a veteran Palestinian nationalist, but a less colourful one. Fatah, on the contrary, as a skilful
underground organization, was intact; it met the Arab need to
do something about the new Israeli presence on the West Bank
and in Gaza, it could put a good face on defeat. As some ultimate
Arab instrument, Fatah found itself suddenly swamped by goodwill, subsidies and weapons, the donations of oil-rich monarchs
and one-party military bosses alike. Fatah set about asserting its
supremacy among Palestinian organizations and by February
1969, after much intricate manoeuvring, Yasser Arafat had been
elected chairman of the PLO Executive Committee. A year later,
a further committee known as the Palestine Armed Struggle
Command, or PASC, gave the impression that a National
Liberation Front had been formed on the Algerian model. This
was not the case. Old unsolved doctrinaire issues continued to
fissure the movement. In order not to repeat Shukeiry's mistakes
Fatah did not define what kind of government Palestine would
have after its liberation and the documents of intention which it
published – for instance the Palestine National Charter of 1969
– were statements of nationalism without ideology which
could not offend the assorted Arab governments whose aid was
indispensable. The PFLP, however, declared that revolutionary
socialism would liberate first the Arab countries and then
Palestine, adapting the former Shukeiry slogan about routing
the road to Tel Aviv through Amman. Habash and Haddad and

their friends were Christians, obliged to act as extremists in pursuit of better credentials as Arabs. If Fatah supporters were the Moslem rank and file, PFLP members tended to be more sectarian and intellectual. After a further split within the PFLP, another factional group emerged, the Popular Democratic Front, under Naif Hawatmeh, a young Christian Bedouin from the East Bank. Hawatmeh accused Habash of bourgeois origins and perhaps was making a Maoist bid.

Except in academic circles none of these controversies and jealousies would have mattered had the *fedayeen* been able to externalize them against Israel. Without a base on the West Bank they could not do so. Although the number of river-crossings rose, guerrilla effectiveness declined. Their last and most notorious big exploit – one more typical of 1948 – was the explosion of a bomb in the Mahane Yehuda market of Jerusalem, in which eleven people were killed. The Israelis erected wire fences with minefields and electronic screens, so that by the end of 1969 their security forces were killing or capturing nine out of ten *fedayeen* on infiltrations, a casualty rate quite out of proportion to gains from sabotage. Besides passive defences, the Israelis were also active in bombing *fedayeen* on the East Bank. Israel was guaranteeing her security by sealing the guerrillas off as solely an internal problem within the Arab world, thus forcing the cruel logic of the position: either King Hussein really was with the *fedayeen* as he told them, in which case Jordan could pay for it, it could even become Palestine if that was what its citizens desired; or else the king had to disown them and save his country, in their words, by betraying the Palestinian revolution.

Briefly the problem was shifted northwards when the *fedayeen*, frustrated in the Jordan valley, tried to attack Israel across its border with Lebanon. The mountains of the Anti-Lebanon offer much better guerrilla prospects than the Jordan valley; they are steep, isolated and have plenty of cover. In response to this development, on Christmas Day 1968 the Israelis landed helicopter-borne troops on Beirut airport to destroy some civil aircraft. The Lebanese government fell and for seven precarious months another could not be formed because the lesson of the Israeli raid was so public – the Lebanese were in the same boat as the Jordanians. For them too it was less of a risk to keep the border quiet than to have the Israelis do it for them. In April 1969 the Lebanese army fought some two thousand *fedayeen* of the Saiqa, a Palestinian group enrolled into the Syrian army, and that October, at the battle of the Rechiya crossroads leading between Israel and Syria, the Lebanese army decisively established its superiority over all *fedayeen*. As a government spokesman put it, 'Do they want to see Lebanon in ruins for the sake of blowing up a few water-pipes in Israel?' The Israeli warnings had been accepted.

If Jordan could be slid over into chaos and the Palestinians did indeed take over the country, the balance of power in the Middle East would alter. The Russians have used the Arab–Israeli conflict to maintain their presence in Egypt and Syria, and so long as instability lasts their interests in the region must remain open-ended. For the Arabs positive results are required from the Russian alliance: the consequences of the Six-Day War must be reversed. Russian pressure for the return of Sinai to Egypt can be clear-cut. But should the West Bank be given back to King Hussein or to the *fedayeen*? So many imponderables are at stake that the Russians have dodged the question by helping the guerrillas very little materially but with a barrage of propaganda. Zionism equals Imperialism equals America equals Aggression equals Nazism: out of this equation has been fashioned the party line on the Middle East and with it the world-picture of those under the sway of scientific socialism. Jordan's annual budget does receive American subsidies, Israel does occupy the West Bank, the *fedayeen* were being opposed – with some shaping and lopping of the context, Palestine could be slotted into the spectrum of Third World causes.

In the mournful years of exile the Palestinians had been neglected or at best patronized, but now supporters fell upon them from all sides. The Fatah and PFLP and PDF offices in Amman were faced with difficulties which would have confused far more experienced politicians: how to take advantage of being so fresh yet so stale a cause, and how to deal with the kind of fad which rides upon the back of the mass media. Television crews descended with the rapacity of carrion-birds. They wanted meat. They shot scenes of Lion Cubs in training. In jeeps with extinguished headlights they were jolted and jarred along dirt-tracks on moonless nights in the Jordan valley; they were provided with a bedding-roll in a hide-out and kept waiting, waiting for a D-Day that had to be postponed, with soaring tension, because already to cross the river into the West Bank was suicide. The Israelis were drubbed and trounced in press releases and communiqués, yet those victories could never be followed up or checked upon. But who could be quite sure about the vague shapes under the trees of Ajloun, the night-flashes or the mortars thudding ahead over the range? Dispatch riders zoomed, dusty unshaven men in combat fatigues lay around exhausted while their commanders in handsome khaki debriefed them and circulated the good news in Ivy League and Oxford accents. In a red and white *keffiyeh* Yasser Arafat was as strikingly elusive as the Scarlet Pimpernel, he could call a press conference in the small hours and count on the wire-services, he was menacing and democratic. A real now-man, he had made the cover of *Time* magazine.

Predicting the demise of Jordan has been a favourite pastime in the Middle East but never so much as between the battle of Karameh and the civil war in September 1970. Already in November 1968 the first serious clash between the army and the *fedayeen* in Amman had left twenty-four dead and eighty-nine injured. Like sparring matches before a prize fight, such bouts recurred regularly, with less and less intervening truce. Curfews were imposed. Prisoners were held and released in the switch-back of politics. Roads to Irbid and Jerash and Kerak were in the hands of the *fedayeen*, the Jordan valley and the Balqa were their fiefs. Apparently unable to get the better of it, the army was supposed to be going over to the *fedayeen* – of all the false-hoods this was likely to be the most damaging. Prime Minister Bahjat Talhouni wavered until his final fall, unsure how to steer the *fedayeen* but unwilling to crush them in the manner of the Lebanese or of his successor, Wasfi Tel.

Whatever was to happen in the region would be decided by the Palestinians for they held the centre of the stage and would never be dislodged – documentaries and articles by the dozen forged such propositions, often illustrated with a photograph posed in a conference salon of King Hussein shaking hands with Arafat. Some new compromise between them had been reached, or would be, only to finish in obscure shooting, the work, it was said, of *agents provocateurs* and undercover men. On either side a promise was as good as an accusation. In February 1970 *The Times* of London was writing of 'the very real possibility that robbed of half his kingdom and with his authority diminishing in that part which remains, the king may decide that it is time to quit'. At round-table conferences throughout Europe professors and lobbyists hammered at the boundaries of a future republican Palestine. Western intellectuals rummaged among their convictions in case Fatah were right-wing and bourgeois, and they debated whether the PFLP or the PDF used terror in a revolutionary or a counter-revolutionary way. Dogmas from France, bromides from Germany, guilt and self-criticism from America.

Revolutionary romanticism – a flower from Asia shipped via South America – attracted some students and they spent a season or two camping out with the *fedayeen*. One of them, a Frenchman, was even killed in an Israeli air-raid. Exoticism carried others beyond their depth, like the prominent English lady who after the usual Fatah guided tour emerged from a cave in the thrall of its *boum* and *ou-boum*, the echo postponed from E. M. Forster's celebrated Marabar Caves. A few believed that only dead Jews would make amends for Israel. Such fans arrived to promote victory after the resistance movement had suffered already the one defeat which counted, on the West Bank. The *fedayeen* did not have to let themselves be driven either into more posturing or into a showdown with the Jordanian army which was certain to be more bloody and final than any number of Karamehs. Secrecy and diplomacy could have given them the necessary options. With publicity, with the party line, they ceased to be Palestinians in need of justice, they became mascots for the cause-mongers over their shoulders, for the cinema teams of modish young bullies with fierce hair and girls in tailored denims, for the anonymous promoters who ride in cars with CD plates, the perpetual expense-account set, those who mount someone else's cause on someone else's money.

4 · Means and Ends

The Israelis were not prepared to take the slightest risk over the internal security of the West Bank. To them the battle of Karameh was part of a continuing process of roll-back which would end, hopefully, in negotiations. Pending a political settlement, their temporary postwar boundaries might stretch out like the Armistice Agreements over nineteen years, long enough for a baby to grow into a soldier. But while the *fedayeen* were rejecting any compromise and favouring the single military solution, the Israelis might have been cynical and devious enough to take them at their word, by allowing them some run of the West Bank. In which case the population would truly have been trapped between Arab terror and Israeli counter-terror, in the predicament which twice already they had sought to avoid. Another mass exodus would certainly have resulted. A few successful guerrilla actions did cause villagers to evacuate, although not permanently. The guerrillas could have been further manipulated into emptying their own land. The Israelis had not allowed the *fedayeen* to expel the population but on the contrary had been allowed by the population to expel the *fedayeen*. In holding the *fedayeen* as far away as possible outside the frontiers, the Israelis were therefore also bringing themselves face to face with 650,000 Arabs on the West Bank and 350,000 in the Gaza Strip. Nothing forceful was going to make either Israelis or West Bankers vanish. Whatever their feelings, they were going to have to put up with one another. There was nothing else for it.

West Bankers were receiving money from Amman to stiffen

their resistance, they were appealed to as Arabs and patriots. Bulletins of military deeds were issued daily in Amman and Beirut – Israeli officers and soldiers killed by the score, equipment destroyed, time-bombs detonated. West Bankers were able to walk out of doors and have a look for themselves. Month by month, the *fedayeen* ceased to be believable on the West Bank, their second coming postponed until further notice. To the Palestinian organizations and their supporters over the river such coexistence was unacceptable. What sort of bulletins were the West Bankers putting out? They came across the open bridge, they had less to complain about than their families in Jordan who were becoming nervous about the political instability there. These had to be the creatures of the Israelis, undermined, paralysed by an alien occupation.

Occupation: the word itself is chill, it carries associations of jackboots and hostages shot at dawn: Lidice and Oradour, Budapest and Prague, the totalitarian machine at its vile grind. The West Bank and Gaza were under occupation. Occupation meant the guerrillas' defeat and the passivity of the occupied territories, and it was therefore real on both sides of the Jordan. Having seen obstacle courses and heard machine-guns in the Ajloun hills, the television crews and correspondents crossed the Allenby Bridge and searched the West Bank for the reverse of the medal, for the occupation. We found a military government. We found military spokesmen to point out newly demolished houses, we found that *fedayeen* suspects were arbitrarily detained. But most of all, we found the West Bankers in a political fork which they were anxious to explain. Nothing they did was certain to be right. If they went out and shot an Israeli, other Israelis would put them in prison for life. If they did not shoot an Israeli, other Arabs might put them in prison for life for collaborating – but which Arabs, and after a war or a negotiation, and how soon? Occupation: it was like bad weather – everything was the fault of the occupation. Everybody said so. The last time I saw Dr Kadri Tuqan he was standing on the steps of his school in Nablus calling out over the heads of the pupils, 'Occupation must go', as if he were the voice of the

West Bank addressing Samaria and beyond.

Throughout 1969 the Russians were under pressure to deliver more than missiles to the Arabs. That April Nasser had declared a war of attrition, and heavy shelling was resumed over the Suez Canal. Israeli aircraft were bombing Egyptian positions in a dangerous escalation. Soon there were as many Egyptian refugees as ever there had been Palestinian. The Russians and their supporters had to insist on Israeli withdrawal, at gunpoint if need be, from the occupied territories, and in the party press and its dependencies, and in particular *Al-Ittihad*, the Israeli–Arabic communist paper, first began to appear new atrocity stories which aimed at presenting this withdrawal as a moral and political imperative. The Israelis were made to appear brutes and racists, committing unimaginable horrors on defence-less Arabs: the party line decreed so, it gave orders that Occupation must now be added to its equation about Imperial-ism, Aggression, Nazism and so on. The cause-mongers and fellow-travellers brought a case ready-made for the Palestinians, and one which had the merit of justifying anything the guerril-las felt like doing on either bank of the Jordan. Terror looks better if directed against terrorists.

What had been done on the West Bank, and how, and why, was open to inspection and inquiry. Israelis from the army and government departments and researchers and mere private citizens kept on trying to take round anyone who wanted to go and see for himself (and lots who did not want to go and see). But what had they *really* done? Secret histories of the occupa-tion were confided to strangers, including Israelis, for of course some of them were among the best listeners, nipping off to the Knesset or to their newspaper to raise a scandal which winged that very day to presidents and ministers and anybody who needed news to reap. In the main, listeners respected the difficulty of the West Bankers' position too much to print the rumours they heard, for these could only rebound and damage the Arabs. So unrealistic had the battle of words become, how-ever, that harm to the Arabs could also be assumed to be harm to the Israelis. *The Times* of London, for example, on 28 October

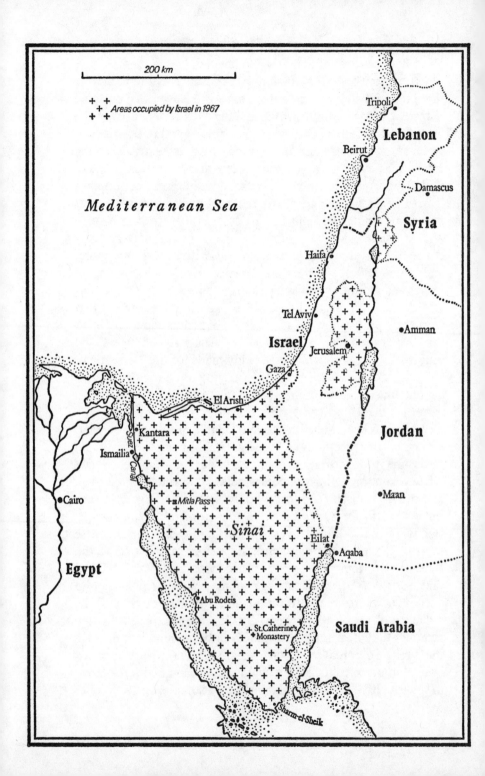

1969 carried an article whose headline typified that moment's play of assertion and propaganda: 'Grim reports of repression in Israel-occupied lands'. As in 1967, in the weeks of war and its aftermath, it was a matter of whom you chose to believe, and, beyond that, to what ends your beliefs could be put.

On the West Bank of the Jordan and in the Gaza Strip (I wrote in the *Sunday Telegraph* of 20 December 1969 and I have shortened but not updated the article here) at present occupied by Israel, a good many people are searching for atrocities, not only journalists from all over the world but every kind of Israeli from right-wing extremists to communists eager for self-accusation.

The atrocity stories start with the incidents in which grenades are thrown or explosive charges are set. The targets for attack are civilians or shops, not military installations, because these are well guarded. The Arab resistance movements try thus to force the hand of the Israelis. After a grenade is thrown, for instance, Arabs on the street are lined up by Israeli soldiers for searching and questioning. Last year in Gaza I happened to see Arabs lined against a wall for just such a search. There was no manhandling but it would not have been surprising if there had been, given the jitters of everyone concerned. A man whom a military tribunal finds guilty of harbouring a Fatah member, or of aiding and abetting resistance, will have his house demolished and some five hundred houses have been blown up.

About eight hundred *fedayeen* infiltrators from Jordan have been killed in armed clashes. Another 2,400, including those who joined West Bank groups, have been captured and are held in Israeli prisons. Nearly half of these have been sentenced, the rest await trial. At present there are also 771 Arabs under administrative arrest, by an old British Mandate regulation allowing for a man to be detained for a six-month period which is renewable.

Any investigator into the question of systematic atrocities will be baffled as he listens to Arab stories and Israeli denials.

'It depends what you mean by torture,' I was told frankly last week by an Israeli general who until a few months ago was one of the senior administrators of the Arab areas. 'Nine out of the ten guerrillas we capture are so frightened that they tell us everything they know. As for the one who doesn't talk, you have only to do like this,' and the general raised his hand as for a back-handed slap, 'and he begins. We have to know if any members of a guerrilla patrol have got away – don't forget they came here to murder Jews or Arabs for whom we're responsible.'

For this visit I began at Kalkilya. The town has been rebuilt since I was last here after the war – the mayor tells me that six families still live in tents. No Israeli is present while we talk. Thirty Kalkilya men are under administrative arrest but the military governor has promised the mayor that they will shortly be released. They have done nothing, the mayor thinks, and nothing has been done to them. His secretary, a young man who has recently been held for three weeks, claims that he was beaten and rolls up his trouser-leg to show me a scar on his shin about the size of a sixpence. If this was from an Israeli kick, I ask, why is the scar-tissue the same brown colour as the rest of his leg? It should be new, pink. He shrugs. It is the first of dozens of such encounters.

In Nablus, Hamdi Cana'an, the mayor until his recent resignation, is convinced that the Israelis are committing every sort of atrocity. For example, his town clerk was caught on the Allenby Bridge carrying a message in his shoe for the Fatah in Amman. Visiting him in prison, Hamdi Cana'an heard that he had been hung up by the wrists for so long that he lost the use of his right arm. Those listening nod. In the office with us is a municipal employee whom the Israelis held for three days of questioning. He was the only man I met in Nablus who spoke moderately as far as he himself was concerned. As for the Fatah, nobody knows a thing about it. 'Our share in the struggle', says Hamdi Cana'an, 'is to suffer.'

It is the same in Gaza. In the military governor's office I hear the official view first. Four weeks ago an Israeli shopkeeper, Shlomo Levy, was murdered in full view of the merchants around. That they did nothing to stop this is taken as connivance and their stalls have been demolished. A curfew has been imposed on Falestin Square and a section of the main street.

'The conception of torture is a pure fantasy,' says the Israeli colonel. 'You've been here often, you must know the Arab mentality.' He describes a school strike of a year ago, during which three girls were hurt by stones and taken to hospital. When he visited them, the colonel says, all the patients in the public wards, with diseases ranging from colds to tuberculosis, shouted at him that they too were the victims of stone-throwing.

Among many examples given by the colonel was the case of a teacher called Fatma Mahmud Afana. While she was being tried, a delegation from the Gaza Advocates' Association came to complain to him that the girl's teeth had been broken and her finger-nails pulled out, and all Gaza knew it. They had only to go down to the court-room to see for themselves that it was not true. 'The facts take the wind out of their sails,' concluded the colonel. In Gaza, I learn from the colonel, *fedayeen* organizers pay anyone a little over one dollar to throw a grenade. The grenade is thrown at a travelling car so that during the four seconds before the explosion the car can drive fifty or eighty yards and is therefore out of range. Why then is the grenade not thrown ahead of the car? The colonel has heard the answer a hundred times: that if the grenade really killed someone, the thrower would be fired on.

At the Municipality I find the Mayor of Gaza, Raghib el-Alami, and his council. They are discussing a letter from the military governor. The curfew will be lifted if the council signs an undertaking: 'We object to all acts of sabotage and will do our best to keep the peace and security.' Although other town councils have signed similar documents, the Gaza one will not because it would lose face with the local population. The curfew stays, the population suffers. Hundreds of people are beaten in the streets, they tell me. One man has witnessed cigarette burns on a sixteen-year-old student from Khan Yunis. Can he give me the name so that I may see for myself? He has forgotten but the boy was known as Prisoner Number 11. But, I object, the Israelis call prisoners by their name and give them no numbers. Silence.

Next day I attend a trial in the military governor's compound at Ramallah on the West Bank. Ahmed Mohammed Assaf is charged with possessing fire-arms and helping others to join an unlawful organization. The women of Assaf's family are sitting in court while other Arabs wait at a sentry post outside. The court is open.

Assaf is being defended by Antun Jaser, of Jerusalem, one of the eleven Arab lawyers willing to accept cases on the West Bank. Afraid of being struck from the Jordanian bar, the other lawyers refuse to appear. Antun Jaser is also the defending lawyer in the case of Bashir el-Khairy, himself an advocate, who told his judges that his confession was extracted under torture. The court adjourned to consider the evidence and has so far not announced any decision. If anything can be substantiated, as Antun Jaser thinks, this case is the only one I came across which might provide a scandal (as the death in prison of Kassim Abu Aker did last year, prompting questions in the Knesset and an official inquiry).

A major and two lieutenants form the tribunal. The prosecutor is a young bespectacled lieutenant called Yossi – 'my very good friend,' says Antun Jaser. They have often met before. Assaf sits next to two Arab policemen armed with rifles. The interpreter switches from Hebrew to Arabic to English. Your Honour and Mr Justice – the formalities are observed. Antun Jaser argues that there is duplicity on the charge sheet. After an hour the court adjourns on the matter.

I take the chance to talk to Assaf, who is a red-faced, thick-set man, in apparent high spirits. He grins. He has confessed the charges. On the prosecutor's table are photographs of the arms found in his house and on exhibit is a clock wired for explosives. Was he tortured? Yes, he says, and to prove it he also pulls up his trouser-leg to reveal the kind of scratch a bramble might make. I bring Yossi in on this, and he looks pained. Like all Israeli soldiers, he says that if there were torture in so small a country he would know about it. 'Very good liars, these Israelis,' whispers Antun Jaser. The torturers, the Arabs claim, belong to the General Security Forces. Sometimes they produce a name, Captain Menaham or Captain Elazar being the most frequently quoted. How do they know the name and rank? They are not sure.

On my way to visit Nablus prison I gave a lift to a young soldier of the Security Forces. He came originally from Morocco, and was far from intelligent. Sometimes they searched houses in daylight, more usually at night, he explained. In nearly all cases they were acting on what an informer had told them, and they nearly always found the weapons they were looking for. Had he ever tortured anyone or seen torture done? 'No.' Would he ever torture if given the order to do so? 'Why not? An order is an order. But I was never given it.'

Outside Nablus prison some families are waiting to see their men. The governor, Captain Golan, shows me round. The prison was once a Turkish *khan*, converted by the British, used by the Jordanians until taken over intact but empty by the Israelis. In round figures here are 300 men under sentences ranging from one week to five years; 150 more awaiting trial and 150 under administrative arrest: 28 women and two children. A staff of 100, half of whom are Druzes, while another quarter are Jews from Oriental countries, who can speak Arabic. With this occupation these Sephardi Jews, many of them rough types, are finding that after years of being underdogs to the Arabs they have become the masters. Their past resentments give rise to much of the Arab–Jewish friction in daily contact.

Warders do not accompany us round these big, high rooms and no guns are carried anywhere in the prison: the governor could easily be assassinated. The men sleep on pallets, with blankets. In spite of the overcrowding, the atmosphere is informal, relaxed.

The governor knows the prisoners by name and discusses their case with them, especially those held under administrative arrest who are anxious for a decision. We walk at a leisurely pace, and I am free to talk to whom I please and go where I want. Several prisoners take me on one side to praise the governor in my ear.

Of course in these circumstances every motive can properly be suspected. I stand in the middle of these rooms, sometimes with seventy or eighty prisoners, asking aloud who was tortured. Many speak English, but the governor translates. Five or six hands go up. Then another five or six. All of these claim to have been beaten in Sarafand prison. Sarafand is a former British camp outside Ramleh in Israel, used for military training. Its name is now Zerifin, and the word Sarafand itself is a Mandate relic.

Patiently the governor tells them that he has received them in this prison direct from interrogation, and none of them has ever been taken inside Israel. They crowd round us, and they are smiling. Soon we discuss real topics. What will they do when they are released? Will they dare tell the Fatah they have been well treated in an Israeli prison? After hesitation many answer that they will go back to their village. Only two men told me that they would return to fight.

The leader of one room is Taysir Kubbeh. In charge of the student section of the Palestine Liberation Organization, he came from Amman to start a student network and was denounced after ten days. He talks with intelligence of his work and political aims. In English he tells the governor that torture takes place during interrogation, and that the governor knows it. Kubbeh is not put out. He is in good humour.

'Look,' answers the governor in English, 'you know it's not true. For many months now I've seen nobody with a single mark on him. About a year ago a very few men captured in a fight had some broken bones, and that's all there's ever been.'

Kubbeh agrees. It is an astounding moment.

In the room next door is the town clerk of Nablus, whom I have been wanting to meet. A slight and bookish man, he says that he has been hung by the wrists for two days, and was then fettered in a cell forty centimetres square. No man could fit into that space – but the crucial fact is that his wrists are completely unmarked, the hairs are thick on them, and his arms are normal. (Unfortunately, when I went back to confront Hamdi Cana'an about this, he was away for the Id-el-Fitr feast. I also wished to quote to him his testimony in the visitors' book that everything was satisfactory.)

Back in his office the governor suggests that I will learn a lot if I see new prisoners brought in, attempting to kiss his boots, Ottoman-style. What about interrogations? 'Last week a Jordanian officer was captured and that afternoon gave away over one hundred men in his resistance groups. They talk, they are frightened. But put yourself in our position. If you knew a terrorist could tell you about an attack, you'd have to get the information, wouldn't you?' The governor's last words to me were 'You are so disappointed when you see these poor people. We would like to teach them to be men.'

Kfar Yona is a maximum security prison in Israel with none of the informality of Nablus. Here is that observance of the letter of the law which friends of Israel admire, but which exasperates its critics. Still no guns inside. The governor comes round, with warders locking doors behind us. The prisoners are crowded here too, they stand up when we come in and say 'Shalom.' Again I ask who has been tortured, but now the men are brought to the governor's office to answer further questions.

Mohammed Hassan Sheik Halil claims to have been beaten on the chest and denied medical attention. His file is brought up with the prison doctor, and we are assisted by Dr Cohen, the elderly Chief Medical Officer of Prisons, who is on inspection. Halil strips. He has an ugly surgical scar on his ribs from a car accident four years ago. He describes the accident. X-rays have shown tubercular scarring on his lungs. His file is thick with medical reports and soon we are discussing his albumen and Wasserman tests. Halil himself is now arguing about what the doctors said last time.

It is a collective hysteria, Dr Cohen thinks. Three patients in his hospital say they have been paralysed by torture. Two teams of nerve and muscle specialists can find nothing wrong.

It is again proper to wonder if this has been specially arranged for me. If so, these doctors must be in the plot. But it is at my request that I am visiting these particular prisons, and my pass, signed by the commissioner of prisons, specifies that I am to have free access and permission to interview any prisoner I please. To ask the governor point-blank if he has fixed things may not be very useful, but I ask all the same.

'The two men you saw in solitary confinement were put there yesterday. I knew you were coming and I could have waited till you'd gone,' is his answer.

One after another the prisoners are brought in, picked by me at random. Fifty per cent here are illiterate, only four per cent have secondary education. One of the latter is Judge Adel Muhamed Shurab from Gaza who would require evidence, he says, before committing himself about torture. Many of the prisoners here describe an electricity treatment and make a gesture of turning a handle, as on an old telephone. I ask what the generator looked like. They do not know. Did the electricity leave marks? Some say yes, some no.

Adel Ibrahim Samra, a student from the university in Beirut, describes his electric shocks as burning. The wires were connected to his ears from a 4½-volt battery. When I ask how so small a battery could have enough power to burn, I notice his hands are trembling uncontrollably. He sees me looking and hides them under the table. Because he and all of them are lying or because they are afraid of answering questions in front of the governor, I ask. No: prison treatment is admitted to be correct.

In a way the strangest feature of this whole investigation is the prisoners' absence of bitterness, or even emotion, almost as if the prisoners were uninvolved, which would be impossible had they really been tortured. According to the Geneva Convention, they may choose whether to wear boots or slippers. A prison survey finds that ninety-four per cent have chosen slippers, which shows a disinclination to escape or fight. Discipline is steady, though sometimes the guards are cursed.

In one of the most quoted chapters of *Seven Pillars of Wisdom* Lawrence generalizes about the character of the Arabs.

This people was black and white, not only in vision, but by inmost furnishing: black and white not merely in clarity, but in apposition. Their thoughts were at ease only in extremes. They

inhabited superlatives by choice. Sometimes inconsistents seemed
to possess them in joint sway; but they never compromised: they
pursued the logic of several incompatible opinions to absurd ends,
without perceiving the incongruity.

A page or two later he concludes with one of those thrusts which
cut through so much of his rhetoric, 'Arabs could be swung on
an idea as on a cord.'

A century ago in her book *The Inner Life of Syria, Palestine
and the Holy Land* Isabel Burton, wife of the great explorer, had
expressed herself on the subject in a more standard English.

In the East it is safer to treat everyone as if he might some day
be your enemy. Nevertheless, it must be said, that when they want
to be enemies, they do not become so on anything that has
happened, or has been said. Out of the very stones they will
fabricate such a tower of falsehoods that you can only stand
and gape in wonder and admiration at their fruitful invention
and audacious unscrupulousness.

Two texts towards a grasp of the Arab–Israeli encounter in its
present stage, though there is more to it than simply deciding
who has most interest in spreading which lies. The tower is
fabricated, as Mrs Burton said, out of the very stones; and out of
stone even an invention turns real. For if the Israelis have to face
the Arabs, the Arabs also have to face the Israelis, stone to
stone, invention to invention. The mutual shock goes very deep,
into the dark and unexplored caverns of personal and national
psyche. For years the Arabs of the West Bank have lived like
patients in some isolation chamber, breathing in the rarefied
ether of revenge and cut off completely from any world outside
their own. What they knew of the Israelis was what they were
left to imagine, for they never saw their enemies in the flesh.
Black and white in vision and in inmost furnishing. They
inhabited superlatives: the Israelis were the wickedest people
in the world, dispossessors and spoilers, and so clever that they
had tricked the entire Arab nation not once but several times.
Also the Israelis were about to be wiped out, they were snakes
for the scotching, other men's dupes, children of the dollar, so

low that they were unworthy opponents. This was to pursue the logic of several incompatible opinions to absurd ends, until one fateful day, with almost no preliminaries, the Israelis acquired human shape.

By rights, by all accounts, by custom, the Israelis should have cut the throats of the young men, they should have dishonoured the women, called upon the elders to denounce Allah, and expelled shattered remnants – a black and white vision easy to believe, and one which would very properly call down revenge on unborn generations for ever. The Israelis did something stranger, and in a way worse. Internment and demolition of houses, however high-handed, was nothing new and only to be expected, almost welcomed as a confirmation that the Jews were really like their image. But what was to be made of the military government's officials who kept on coming to insist that the Arabs would be left alone and unharmed if they left the Israelis alone and unharmed? And that being the case, they returned with experts who liked to drink coffee and offer their services, making suggestions for mundane improvements to do with crop-yields per dunam, irrigation, marketing and credit facilities. They were conquerors no doubt but they were also worried little men in open-necked shirts and the cheapest of machine-sewn trousers, men who looked as if they were perpetually about to make a gaffe, or might bite their finger-nails. Their goodwill was something like an unsolicited gift on a doorstep, difficult to accept or reject. The comforting old ether of revenge was not adequately supplied by these people. Raising questions in their mind about the nature of the Israelis, the West Bankers lost confidence in themselves. For if the Jews were not utter abominations but prepared, even though on their own terms, to be helpful, what had the Palestinians been living through all these years but hopes and beliefs which sprang from false premises? To shatter a people's estimation of themselves has nothing physical about it but may be a torture just the same.

The awakening of guerrillas to Israeli reality was even more fraught. Equipped with might and right, they penetrated into occupied territory which was their very own. The shooting-match was over in a few minutes, and suddenly the survivors were in the hands of those they had come to kill. Everything must go into reverse: heroes are humbled, the brave have been out-braved, the merciless are in need of mercy. So inferior yet so superior, so hateful yet so powerful, the enemy stands plain, his jeeps pluck away freedom, his investigators are speaking Arabic and already primed with intelligence. That scene which I had refused to witness in Captain Golan's room in Nablus gaol would be enough to collapse many a personality: imagine throwing yourself at the governor's feet and being ordered to stand up and act like a man.

On the face of today's world, torture appears to be inherent in any clash between security forces and guerrillas, and there is no reason why Israel should differ from all countries which have practised it as a counter-insurgency weapon. Since the Israelis need information from the *fedayeen*, stories of torture are entirely to their advantage, predisposing prisoners into a panicky belief that they will be broken by interrogators who stick at nothing (so much so that some stories sound as if they have been helped on their way by the Israeli secret service). Yet setting out to substantiate what I could, I had the feeling of *déjà vu*. I had done all this before, I had trailed back and forth on the roads, from pillar to post, trying to nail the atrocity rumours of 1967. As before, questions and answers never quite met. The shapes of the conversations, their decorative quality, were more instructive than facts. Asked point-blank if they were torturers, some Israeli soldiers and officials went through patient refutations about how impossible it was for them to maltreat Arabs what with a judicial process, law-courts, military discipline, their moral prohibitions. Others were insulted, and became rude. One could learn from them about human character. And always one more interview: the hundredth Israeli colonel or the hundredth Arab, adding to the weight of words repeated so very often without the missing clue.

By now I have learnt extra details: for instance, that an Israeli interrogator has been dismissed for stepping outside permitted guide-lines. Which recalls the general's gesture of the back-handed slap. Perhaps such an interrogator may strike and kick an Arab prisoner, stand him up against a wall, confront him with hooded informers, keep him awake at night while guard-dogs bark in the courtyard, and get away with it. On what scale is it torture for a warder to push a man along a corridor or into a truck? Fundamentally, Western rationalism provides no appropriate answer. To the Westerner conclusions are the end-results of facts. To him the torture stories must be either true or false, factually, and having ascertained which is the case he can distribute praise or blame accordingly and become a moralist with a clear conscience. It never occurs to him that these Arab torture stories are, in Lawrence's phrase, the logic of several incompatible opinions pursued to absurd ends, and can there-fore be true and false at the same time. 'Sometimes inconsistents seemed to possess them at once in joint sway.'

A cultural gap has to be spanned. It hardly matters whether the torturings of *fedayeen* prisoners are any more objectively true or false than the rumours of atrocities to refugees in 1967. The confrontation of the Arabs with Israel is not some sensation about prison sadism, it is a profound issue. People's identities are at risk. The Arabs are a shame-oriented people and they have lost face; they consider themselves to have been robbed by the Israelis of that due pride and self-respect which every man owes to himself. Many of the tortures of which the Israelis stand accused have historical associations of humiliation for the Arabs, and have been transposed out of wholly Arab customs into the present. For example, the Israelis are supposed to beat prisoners on the head until a wound forms and hair falls out. This very process is one described in *Seven Pillars of Wisdom* as 'the ancient and curious nomad penance of striking the head sharply with the edge of a weighty dagger again and again till the issuing blood had run down to the waist-belt. It caused pain-ful but not dangerous scalp wounds, whose ache at first and whose scars later were supposed to remind the defaulter of the bond he had given.'

Techniques of lie-detecting and drugs would be more efficient than beating a man's head or hanging him by the wrists but there is no mention of them. Electric shocks, the gesture of turning the handle of some generator, are the only halfway concessions to modernity – nobody can imagine a technology beyond his usual terms of reference. Testimonies of torture are unvarying catalogues in which the Arab is portrayed in physical degradation before the Israeli according to his traditional standards. Almost without exception there is a sexual passage in which the victim's manhood is insulted, his genitals abused sometimes to the point of ejaculation. 'The motions of a homosexuality act is enacted by a certain Negro brought specially for this purpose.' The quotation is from a memoir by As'ad Abdul Rahman but this image and the fear that goes with it can be found in plenty of *fedayeen* literature.

Like a poem or a novel, these testimonies have an internal truth. As symbolic representations of the Arab condition, they are the stones of the tower of invention in which the Arabs really are living. The Westerner who presses his logic and his pedantic cross-examinations is assaulting that tower, lifting its stones away as the material of make-believe. So hands begin to tremble, and the prisoners to plead, not angrily, not indignantly, never telling him to go to hell with his doubts. They do not tear him or the cheerful governor to pieces, they smile in that peculiar uninvolved manner. Impotence, shame, the plight of hard Israeli walls of real stone, are converted into fantasies of heroism and endurance, and they retreat behind these defences to live at last as men as they and the governor want. They have been delivered to the enemy who delivers them back to themselves to make what they can of it – that is the drama of their ordeal.

The Westerner too is stuck with the stories he is told and those he tells himself. In Kfar Yona prison there was a dwarf who had struggled to keep up with a Fatah patrol until he was caught far behind the actual clash. His face twisting with rage, he said that he longed to get out just to kill Jews. And the governor was served coffee by an attendant, an Israeli trusty with a concentration camp tattoo on his wrist. Having survived Auschwitz this man could not adjust to anything else; he had turned himself into a prisoner in perpetuity. A malevolent Nibelung, a Man in the Iron Mask: two obsessions, two extremes. Later, on the road to Jerusalem, I stopped outside the entrance to Sarafand thinking that if I stayed there long enough and Arab prisoners were in fact being brought in, I should see the black marias. The road is lined with whiskery cypresses, the bougainvillea climbs among them magnificently. At the camp gate is a red and white barrier. Soldiers passed to and fro. I sat. Then a three-ton truck swerved past off the main road, roared up, the barrier was raised for it without a password, and as the truck shot by I saw that its back was screened. Why the speed, why the screen? In a flash I was sure that this was the vital evidence of conspiracy which I had been searching for — so Arabs must be here after all. I was rooted to the spot, I could not leave although it grew dark and there was nothing but the barrier, the sentry's hut, some girls being whistled at across the road. I too had fantasies of rescue and dramatic exposés. I had my notebooks with me and knew them to be full of the contradictions I had been examining. Common-sense ebbed back, and yet, like Lawrence's Arabs, I had been swung on an idea as on a cord.

5 · *Making Out*

'This stone was laid by Sir Steuart Spencer Davis Kt, CMG.' In 1931, records the same inscription on the front of the Municipality office, Raghib El-Nashashibi, CBE was Mayor of Jerusalem. Teddy Kollek, once of Vienna and of Kibbutz Ein Gev on the eastern shore of Lake Galilee, is mayor now. Past the Municipality, with a skyline glimpse of cupolas and onion-domes from the Russian Compound which is mostly converted into a police headquarters, out on to the Jaffa Road, round the corner of the Barclay's Bank DCO, and there – lizard-grey in the sun – are the walls of the Old City. The view is unthinkable. Everybody feels under the skin that this is a military zone, that the Arab Legion soldiers keep ghostly watch at their old sandbag-posts upon those walls. The houses around are battle-scarred, some of them boarded. The fortress-convent of Notre Dame de Sion gapes with shell-holes, its holy statue on the roof rises as white and straight as an artillery marker. The traffic hoots and thrusts across noman's land. Once the only contact was at the Mandelbaum Gate where every morning two corporals would exchange their national newspapers and salute in a ceremony which might have been devised in the more formal days of Sir Steuart Davis Kt, CMG. Now the old hands have to remember where the Mandelbaum Gate actually was. Divided Jerusalem was two backwaters, two frontier cul-de-sacs away from their hinterlands. One would climb Mount Zion and peer down at the far-off mystery of Arab buses with ant-sized passengers – or on the Arab side gaze up at the Israeli presence above and wonder at its invisibility and weight.

United again, Jerusalem becomes its mixed provincial-cosmopolitan self, as it was in the Mandate. Unity – annexation. The Arabs of East Jerusalem are Palestinians with Jordanian nationality and Israeli citizenship and residence. They have Jordanian passports and are provided for the time being with special travel papers and Israeli identity cards. They pay taxes at the Israeli rates, including municipal taxes, and in return they get better services than before, although on their electricity bills is the special levy applied to Israelis for defence purposes. In Jerusalem the books and curricula of Arab schools in Israel have to be used, although for entry into Arab universities pupils will need the Jordanian or Egyptian *tawjihi*, or matriculation, and not a certificate from Israel. Hundreds of children from well-known Jerusalem schools like the Rashidiya and the Mamouniya are now sent by their parents elsewhere on the West Bank.

In the old days in Palestine there used to be a fever, a sort of quinsy, and someone with it would have to stay in bed for a bit. Asked how he felt, he would reply '*Kolubuja*' (as I shall choose to spell it) or 'Everything hurts.' The Arabs are in the grip of *kolubuja* fever and the bedside manner of the foreigner tends to bring out symptoms. The continuing metaphor of convalescence is not out of place. The first to pick up were those connected with tourism. In the summer of 1971 some 106,000 Arabs arrived across the Allenby Bridge to visit their relations. They swamped facilities and politics alike. Staying up to three months, they had the chance to see at first-hand this occupation of the West Bank. The teenagers hitch-hiking to the Dead Sea or to Tel Aviv were likely to be students from Damascus or Kuwait. They and their families would be eating out in Israeli restaurants and buying jeans or electric toasters in Israeli shops. Thousands of weekenders made the beach at Natanya their favourite spot and for reasons of modesty Arab women would bathe there fully dressed, like big Portuguese men-of-war as their clothes billowed about in the water. Not a single act of sabotage was reported as a result of these summer visits, and that in itself may bring on a bout of *kolubuja* fever. On the one hand West Bankers want to see their relations from the Arab world, but on the other hand they feel that the tranquillity of the whole business may earn them a bad reputation.

Tens of thousands of West Bankers work across the Green Line of the Armistice. Nobody seems to know for sure how many, nor on what basis membership of the Histadrut or Israeli Trade Union Federation is arrived at, with all that this implies in rights, guaranteed wage-levels, sickness benefits, pensions. Every day at first light buses and lorries rumble along to recognized places (like the YMCA and Peter Nasr's sports ground in East Jerusalem) and deposit the labourers. Some Israelis require casual workers for a day or a week, and they simply collect them in their Chevrolet pick-up or whatever. The great majority of the workmen, however, have steady jobs in factories and on construction sites: they are contributing their labour to the Israeli economy, and they do not care, for these are men who never before had regular employment at such pay, and for whom a new suit or a pair of children's shoes would be once-in-a-lifetime extravagances.

Kolubuja again: the Jews are providing for the Arabs the jobs and cash they cannot provide for themselves. Out of self-interest, it can be said, because starving Arabs with nothing to lose would become guerrillas, and these Jews are too clever for that. Yet those who sit in a lawyer's office or a decent home on the West Bank and criticize the Arab labourers for a deficiency of revolutionary spirit are in the invidious position of the rich blaming the poor. They can afford their criticism, especially when they get their hands on funds from Amman or more indirectly from the Israelis. Besides, time is passing – and who are they to be more radical than the hundred thousand visitors and the fifty thousand labourers? Unless they look sharp, they will be outwitted. Most of the merchants along the streets were agents for European firms, they have their clients, and now the Israeli salesmen have taken to calling regularly, offering contracts, stock, partnerships. Chances are in the present. Money is for the making.

On Al-Zahra Street in East Jerusalem a new branch of the Hapoalim Bank is opened and is busy. Over the way the Arab

Bank is closed. Opposite is Marwan Assali's bookstore, a centre of good conversation. Next to it is the shop and agency of Mohamed Dajani whose empty house in no-man's land was illegally occupied by an Israeli whom he sued successfully for eviction in a *cause célèbre*.

'You're Christian? Shake on it.' This pimp whom I cannot get rid of claims to be a schoolboy and to have a special line in some *parti carré*. He works outside the National Palace Hotel. Anybody with social pretensions drops in there for a coffee or a cold drink during the morning. Musa Alami has his suite and lives like the uncrowned king that he is, protected by his sense of style and his lawyer, Dr Maz'uz. Musa Alami is from one of the most notable of Jerusalem families. An old man now, Musa Alami was a Mandate official in the legal department before he ran the Arab Office to promote the Palestine case in the years leading to the 1948 war. He is the author of one of the two or three penetrating Arab studies about that war.

Afterwards he persuaded the Jordanian government to give him land in the Jordan valley and down near Jericho he started his Arab Development Society, a farming project which provided work for refugees and a home for lots of orphan boys. The farm was a private enterprise version of a kibbutz; it was wrecked by refugees once before 1967 and since then it has been hit by a guerrilla rocket or two. Musa Alami stayed away for a while but he is back to supervise it, and drives down there in mid-morning. Recently he appeared on Israeli television to reminisce, for he has seen it all and met everybody from the First High Commissioner to Ben Gurion. On this programme he called the Military Governor of Ramallah, Colonel Feldman, 'a perfect gentleman'. A phrase like that springs from cherished cultural depths, it sweeps the present as clean as a breeze.

Also to be met on the terrace of the National Palace is Hazem Khalidi, a former British officer and a portly figure in a bow-tie. He is arranging to restore the famous Khalidi Library in the Old City, which has been shut since 1948. Down the road lives Anwar Nusseibeh, former Jordanian Ambassador in London. One of his brothers has been a minister in Jordan, another is a large contractor. He was secretary of the Arab Higher Committee in Jerusalem, and lost a leg in 1948. An elderly uncle of his is introduced to me as the nephew of Haj Amin, the mufti; he speaks an exquisite turn-of-the-century French. In the garden at the back of Anwar Nusseibeh's house is a wreathed tomb which he built to some Jordanian soldiers killed in the Six-Day War. Next door is the Nusseibeh family office, another handsome Turkish-style building which received a direct hit through the roof but is being restored. And how they work at it, all day long, without tea-breaks, untiringly handing the tiles up in a wicker basket. Anwar Nusseibeh speaks as an Englishman might. 'One loves one's country, one hopes,' he says of the political attitudes of the West Bankers. 'One doubts that anything good could emerge from this occupation.' One of his sons has spent the summer working on a kibbutz.

Anwar Khatib was the *mutaserrif*, or Governor of Jerusalem. He has a lithe, almost athletic manner, he is impeccable in a pinstripe suit, and has well-bred freckles. His present office is on Saladdin Street. We sit in spongy leather armchairs, the room fills, the morning's audience is social yet finicky with plays within plays. Although a Palestinian Anwar Khatib, like Anwar Nusseibeh, is held to be King Hussein's man, but in reserve, as it were, as one of this small group of influential loyalists who might some day be figure-heads or a great deal more. He happens also to be the son-in-law of Sheikh Ali Ja'abari of Hebron. After the war he signed a protest against the annexation of Jerusalem. The Israelis drove to his house at midnight and took him off to a hotel in Safad where for a few weeks he had to report to the police three times a day. Now Shlomo Hillel, the Minister of Police, comes to him at regular intervals, and General Dayan too, and indeed anyone who wants to sound out a particular sort of opinion. Anwar Khatib says that he is afraid mostly of Jewish expansion. Actually he wishes that the Israelis were severe and tyrannical so that the population would rise against them – Arab labourers should not be constructing Israel. The bridges should be closed, the issue should be forced, never mind the misery. We smile, we speculate.

Making Out

A member of the Tuqan family enters, a young man who lives in Amman and has just resigned from the diplomatic service. He was secretary in the Jordanian Embassy in Cairo when Anwar Khatib was ambassador. An embarrassing time because every day the radio filled the air with Ahmed Shukeiry's diatribes against Jordan. On the first anniversary of Nasser's death – which is just a few days away – Anwar Khatib will publish a long eulogy in *El-Quds*. Now there is much embracing and recalling of good old days. Next to me sits Ahmed Afifi, the Managing Director and Chairman of the Board of Directors of the Jordanian Jerusalem District Electricity Company, as his calling card puts it. He has the wearied but expressive face of an effendi. He talks about diesel generators and how his company has the concession for Hebron but cannot meet its increasing load. He is also chairman of the private company which built the Ambassador Hotel where the Israeli civilian administration of the West Bank is housed. With the tourist boom, he wants more rent from them, more compensation. For a moment the talk is general, while Anwar Khatib and the Tuqan cousin discuss how many Israelis there really are: five million at least, they guess, if the statistics were not thoroughly faked.

The Rivoli Hotel, the Ritz, the Paradise, Palmyra, the Cleopatra, the names on and around Saladdin Street have the touch of absent glamour. In a radius of a few hundred yards are the offices – just like Anwar Khatib's though not so well appointed – where the West Bank's public opinion is shaped. Only a handful of men have authority enough to say aloud what they think and only a slightly larger number have position enough to be their audience. A few opinion-makers are conspicuous by their absence, deported to Amman for encouraging more than passive resistance. Some of them were traditionalists like Ruhi Khatib, the last Arab Mayor of Jerusalem, no relation of Anwar Khatib's and not to be confused with him either by name or office; or Sheikh Abdel Hamid Sayeh, acting President of the Moslem Supreme Council, whose place has been filled by a member of the Alami family. Others were left-wing or communist politicians like Kemal Nasser or Fayek Mohammed Warrad who had been extending the scope of their previous Jordanian underground activities. Political groupings in East Jerusalem, even if at loggerheads, have something personal about them, the intimacy of staying together on behalf of self and family, with ideology far behind.

Occupation has enlarged the compass to include those with solutions and grievances, balancing ideas and ambitions: Judge Taysir Cana'an (cousin of Hamdi Cana'an of Nablus); Husni al-Ashab, former Director of Education in Jerusalem, who was once responsible for a thousand teachers. In October and November 1967 he was held in Ramleh prison. Ratib Rabi, headmaster of the Rashidiya school. Mohsin Abu Mezer, a Jerusalemite lawyer, was imprisoned in Jordan at the time of the Ali Abu Nuwar coup in 1957, and afterwards edited the Ba'athist newspaper in Damascus. He describes himself as an Arab Nationalist. Like Anwar Khatib he was taken from home and exiled for a while at his own expense in a hotel in Tiberias. The Israelis must end the occupation, he says, and the logic of hardworking history will do the rest; it will dispose of a nineteenth-century Jewish dream and it will democratize the Hashemites. The time has come for the Palestinians to do their bit of annexing.

Openings for advancement are obvious. The *fellahin* are going to labour exchanges, catching the bus, pocketing their Israeli wages – anyone may speak in their names, and who knows, perhaps they will want what he wants. *Al-Basheer* is an Arabic fortnightly paper which belongs to Ibrahim Handel, a businessman from Bethlehem. It attracts young men who would never have got a hearing in Jordanian times but now appear on Israeli television, say what they like, and have the foreign reporters copying it all down. Loosely they form a group known as the Palestine National Alignment and they have pressed for elections as a first step on the high road to glory. Again who knows, perhaps one day somewhere out of this cluster of Saladdin Street offices, in front of cheering crowds, will step a Palestinian president, or another Jordanian governor or some astonishing Israeli-elected Palestinian Knesset members.

El-Quds comes out daily, and with plenty of advertisements and a circulation of around 20,000 it is the chief public forum for the Arabs. Its offices are in fine stone and on the same street as the Habash Grocery which belongs to a cousin of George Habash of the PFLP. The newspaper's proprietor is Mahmud Abu Zuluf, from Jaffa, a tall, sprawling man, and rich. Among the family properties he would like to reclaim, he says, is a former citrus grove which has been developed into central Tel Aviv between Dizengoff and King George Street, and would be worth millions. Before the Six-Day War Abu Zuluf published *Al-Jihad*. In March 1967 the Jordanian government amalgamated *Al-Jihad* into a paper it could control, *Al-Difaa*, which is itself now closed. Abu Zuluf had also been appointed by Shukeiry to the PLO General Assembly and he likes to describe its meetings in the Intercontinental Hotel in Amman or in Gaza. His stories are all that a journalist's should be, very much to the point. After the war he crossed the bridge to inform the Jordanian prime minister that he was starting up a newspaper in Jerusalem. He had already made the investment in plant, he had a licence from the Israelis, he was as independent from them as from the Jordanians or the *fedayeen*. The prime minister, Abu Zuluf says, advised him not to begin printing as within a month the West Bank would be recovered.

Criticizing Abu Zuluf is something of an Arab pastime, and *El-Quds* answers in kind, in a sense banging together the heads of the Israelis and the Jordanians. The paper's chief editorial writer has been Mahmud Abu Shilbaya, a chubby forty-five year old. Recently he has moved to *El-Anba*, the official Israeli–Arabic paper. He was educated in Cairo and has lived in the refugee camp of Aqabat Jaber near Jericho. He has translated into Arabic Edgar Snow's *Red Star Over China*. Five years of his life have been spent in Jafr, most notorious of Jordanian prisons, away in the desert towards Saudi Arabia, and where he met George Habash. He has been variously labelled a socialist and a communist. His friends are like-minded left-wing Palestinians such as Ibrahim Bakr and Kemal Nasser and in other circumstances Abu Shilbaya might have joined with them in the PLO or whatever. Instead he has stayed in Jerusalem to appeal to

Arabs and Israelis alike for a Palestinian state on the West Bank. *No Peace without a Free Palestinian State* is the title of his book, one which gives away the single direction of his argument. He compares it to Herzl's Utopian vision for the Jews. The first print order of 5,000 was sold out, which suggests that he has an audience. Fatah dug its grave by rejecting any Palestinian entity and any political settlement, and he does not think that it can recover from this mistake. In spite of the occupation perhaps Israel can do for the Palestinians what King Hussein patently cannot – he argues the case on television, he thinks that Israelis have open minds and a democracy which Arabs should utilize. The first person to utter such things in public, he has displayed uncommon courage. 'To my friend David Pryce-Jones,' he inscribes a copy of his book, 'hoping that my people will get a real peace.'

The nuances, the *kolubuja*, change. News and views are either as dampening as a sudden rainstorm in the face, or else brilliantly warm and hopeful. The BBC, Kol Israel, Radio Amman, on the hour every hour add a spoonful or two of fertilizer to the grapevine. The commander of the Palestine Liberation Army is being replaced in Damascus; the wife of Yahya Hammoudia, who succeeded Shukeiry, has been refused an entry visa to the West Bank; another Nahal settlement on the Golan Heights; plots and portents. Everybody must be attentive not to lose footing, while they are also addled with indecision.

Out at the end of Saladdin Street is the Jordanian army building into which the Israeli military government has moved. One or two Israelis are sometimes sitting and joking on its steps. A scruffy rope and a slouching soldier in a helmet bar entry. On the top flies the blue and white flag and it can be glimpsed from the office windows above the pines and low-pitched Jerusalem roofs; it is always in the background and flaps to every passing wind.

Almost two years have gone by since I saw Antun Jaser. It is evening when I call on him in the Sanduqa Building near the Sharia Court, and the shutters have been pulled down. Only a barber is at work in the back of his shop, lathering an uplifted chin. Outside a merchant on a stool runs beads through his hands. People go home early. Antun Jaser remembers my *Sunday Telegraph* article extremely well; he jabs an accusing finger, he has been particularly upset by the observation that one scratch looked as if it had been made by a bramble. 'You wrote many bad things about the Arabs.' It is truth I am after, I tell him, truth stripped of propaganda. With lies there can be no understanding, and on that we agree. He bears me no grudge. He thinks that I must have been seduced by the Israeli girl who accompanied me to the court-room. That girl was a lieutenant from the military spokesman's office; she was self-righteous, somewhat unwashed, and read a book throughout the court proceedings. Truth indeed! Do I suppose that they invite lawyers and reporters to gather round when they set about extracting confessions? He has defended over two hundred guerrillas and says that they have been tortured, every one, without exception, not just slaps but real maltreatment – and I am back on a familiar treadmill.

He gives me to read Section 111 in a Government of Palestine Decree, 'the Defence (Emergency) Regulations 1943. As amended until 2 March 1947. Price 250 mils.' 'A Military Commander may by order direct that any person shall be detained in such place of detention as may be specified by the Military Commander in the order.' Take his client of the moment, Bashir el-Khairy. Have I read the court report on the case published in *El-Quds* on 24 October 1969 by Abdul Halim Ghazal? It's all in there, how they took Bashir to Sarafand, stood on his chest, beat him 'down below' till his manhood was lost, kept him in a cell eighty centimetres square with a sewer running below it. He made a secret mark to prove he had been there and he wants the court to adjourn to show it to them. But the Israelis deny altogether that he was in Sarafand and will not adjourn there. Here is his proof. Of course he cannot reveal where the secret mark is or the Israelis would obliterate it.

Antun Jaser was born in a village thirty miles away and describes himself as a lapsed Catholic. During the Six-Day War he sat in the garage of his house at Beit Hanina, along with the wife and two children of a Jordanian minister. No complaint, nothing was done against civilians, nobody was expelled: he wrote and told his friends in America so. 'I must say the Israelis fought a very good war.' Then how are these same people suddenly transformed into sadists? From fear of the *fedayeen* and to prove their powers. To kill the innocent and to torture the guilty are equally barbaric. The Israelis suspected that he had taken money from George Habash and they have been snooping. The Military Governor of Ramallah cleared his name and he gives him his due. 'Some of the Israelis are very good men, of excellent character in every way.' We step into the real daily grievances of high taxation and red tape. Studying in Egypt, his nephew has married a Coptic girl who came here and had her passport stamped. Her visa has run out but she cannot return to the Arab world with that Israeli incrimination in purple ink.

Bashir el-Khairy has confessed to aiding and abetting in the Supersol explosion at the end of February 1969, in which two shoppers in a supermarket were killed by a bomb camouflaged as a tin, and several more were injured. Because of Bashir's claims of torture, the court has gone into what is called 'a petty trial' or a case within a case. Witness after witness has been summoned over interminable months but now at last the judges are going to decide whether the confession stands as admissible evidence or not.

So I return to Ramallah with Antun Jaser and two friends of his from America, one of them a Mr Khouri. We pick up an el-Khairy cousin who is another advocate for the defence. The Ramallah Military Governor's compound is one of a score of buildings in Palestine known as Taggart forts after the designer, Sir John Taggart, who also built a security fence along the borders during the 1936 Arab revolt. The fort is shabbily functional in a style to win the approval of British ministerial committees; it is chunky, ochre in colour. To one side a derelict machine-gun has been mounted by the Jordanians as some trophy. This morning the entrance is unguarded. We amble up and into the corridor, along to the mess where a typical NAAFI waitress serves tepid fizzy drinks. Antun Jaser buys a round of them; he knows everybody here, he is one of the boys, he slaps their backs and they slap his. The presiding officer is late, and we are waiting in the courtyard in a mixed group swapping the latest chestnuts, which are mostly from the Bible, but improved on. One of the legal advisers is a young Israeli from Montreal who shows me the files of the case. Books on preparing explosive found in Bashir's room. Typewriter key comparisons for the leaflets he drafted. His address book and diaries with dates and comments, the Hebrew translations pinned to the original Arabic entries. Confessions by the page, in his handwriting. Here is a long account of how a girl called Rashimiya got in touch with him because she wanted to perform an act (which is always the euphemism). So she came with a box of such-and-such a size, and they met in the Ramallah public library. That was the first contact. Here is a chapter about an aunt in Gaza who is very bourgeois and has nothing good to say about the *fedayeen* organizations.

The young man from Montreal is earnest, the type to worry, to say that the business of putting Arabs through military courts is bad enough without having torture charges thrown in on top. Fortunately there is no death penalty in Israel. 'Jaser's the best lawyer they've got,' he says, 'I'd do just the same if I was him.' With so much blaming and denunciation, the Arabs have to protect themselves from the risk of being retried one day by their fellows. Listening in, Antun Jaser lights another of his thick cigars and answers that Bashir as a lawyer would not incriminate himself voluntarily.

The presiding officer at last arrives in a shower of apology. Bashir is brought in with the other accused, Abdel Hadi Audeh of Bir Zeit, and Khalil Abu Khadijeh. They greet their families, and one of them kisses his mother's hands. The sisters weep. Bashir's father is blind, an old man in a tarboosh, who has to be led up to his son and then sits wiping his eyes. The police major leaves the court and Antun Jaser calls 'Goodbye and don't come back.' The Israelis and the Arab police in the room guffaw and shake and tell each other what good form the lawyer is in.

Indeed he soon dominates, quoting the Palestine Law Reports, *Rex v. Sykes*, Archbold, Kantorowicz. The presiding officer knows it too, he gives a masterly run-down of the Sykes judgement. He and Antun Jaser are in their element.

In a recess I talk to Bashir and the other two. Bashir has a quiet, droopy appearance, more student than terrorist. He repeats what I knew from Antun Jaser. As usual it is not an accusation, nor a demonstration, but a plea, somehow as if I could be a pen-friend or a tolerant uncle. The other two are openly smiling, pleasant to a point which might be ingratiation or mockery. I ask Mr Khouri what he thinks of it, and he rolls his eyes up, spreads his arms wide and launches into a saga about how he bought the police chief of Biloxi, Mississippi, for twenty-five dollars.

No more. The court proceeds. Again, as before, I have found the component pieces of the drama coming unstuck in my hands. The scale is too small, the cause too aberrant, the deaths of two shoppers in a supermarket is so random and futile that nothing can be made of it – the court wears itself away by this patience and thoroughness. Once more motives, events, consequences, become transparent in that white-washed room. I can visualize Rashimiya and her box, that furtive rendezvous in the public library, the courage which is so self-defeating. They must go through with it knowing neither quite why nor whether the murder of others is not the murder of themselves. Confession can consummate such an act, and give it the meaning it must have, not for them, but for the Israelis. Actually confession makes no difference except to them; it may reconcile being linked for a lifetime to two shoppers blown to bits in a supermarket. The evidence fills several fat buff folders on the table. The blind father dabs with a big silk handkerchief at his cheeks, and Bashir and his two friends look bored, sleepy. I cannot bear to be pitying what could not be otherwise, so sad, so meagre. As I slip out, Antun Jaser is returning valiantly to *Rex v. Sykes*. On the outer wall of the Taggart fort, under shadows, is an old English letter-box, painted red, with its inscription GR VI. Like the Jerusalem Municipality foundation stone laid by Sir Steuart Davis, it is in its way the secret mark upon the land, as much as anything Bashir el-Khairy might have hoped to leave among the Israelis.

6 · *Safe on Canaan's Side*

Shimon Peres is Minister of Transport but has a special responsibility for the Palestinian refugees. In Tel Aviv his office on Shaul Hamelekh Boulevard is in a downtown spread of concrete-walled blocks. The ante-room has a table model of an airport, its runway complete with baby bombs on a toy loader. He himself sits at the top of a table large enough for mammoth conferences. In his opinion something should have been done to settle the refugee problem years ago. After the civil war in Jordan plans can reach beyond security measures – all quiet on the Western Bank. No question of anything except cooperation, and Mr Peres wants a lot of it. Some members of the cabinet refuse to integrate the West Bank and Israeli economies; they have authorized an Arab–Israeli industrial park at Erez on the edge of the Gaza Strip but so far not another one at Kalkilya. On a limited budget of about eight million Israeli pounds raised from private sources, Mr Peres set up the grandiosely named Economic Development and Refugee Rehabilitation Trust to fill gaps in the government's sixty-one million pound programmes of camp renewal, health service and vocational training in the occupied areas.

On the West Bank the nineteen camps are small and close to towns. The 63,000 people who live in them have settled, they remain in their families, and from the Israelis they ask for jobs, dispensaries, schools, roads, electricity, which can all be provided. The line between refugees and inhabitants on the West Bank has been disappearing so fast that soon it will cease to exist. In Gaza the eight refugee camps number about 162,000 or not far from half the population (of course thousands more refugees have managed to lead a life outside the camps altogether). They have had a per capita income of a hundred dollars a year. Over-crowding and poverty would breed violence even without politics. Resettlement, however tactful, however expensive, has international implications, and Mr Peres ponders on them: UNRWA, which spends fifty million dollars a year here and employs 10,000 Arabs, is a welfare state of its own, it has tentacles of power, it perpetuates the famous refugee mentality, it will have to go eventually and its funds perhaps more usefully spent over in Jordan.

That evening I meet a Jerusalem journalist and we pick over the latest blooms of gossip on the grapevine. Forty-eight hours later I discover from the local press that Mr Peres is reported to be advocating the immediate end of UNRWA and that I have become what readers know as a reliable authority.

UNRWA headquarters are past the Ambassador Hotel on the outskirts of East Jerusalem, in a large depot of open space and warehouses with the slack impersonality of any barracks. The officials to whom I speak have clipped out the newspaper report about Mr Peres and UNRWA but they are too brimful of indignation for me to confess what has happened. I am to be escorted to the Area Office at Ramallah where the area manager, Mr Bakerjian, will receive me.

The road carries on past Ramat Eshkol and French Hill where new housing estates have been built on requisitioned land. 'Top of the Capital. A New Concept in Modern Living,' as the bill-board announces. Away to the north on the slope of scrub behind Beit Iksa veers a crane. White scars are cutting the rock where the housing project called Nebi Samwil is beginning, in the hands of an Arab contractor from Ramallah. At Beit Hanina, the Nusseibeh family firm is putting up some eighty units. Where the road widens into dual carriageway is the skeleton of a palace which King Hussein did not have time to complete before the war – on the hilltop where King Saul is supposed to have dwelt. Below are the villas of the rich, of Anwar Khatib, of Kotub the millionaire, of Abu Halib in America, of Dajanis and Nashashibis and the rest of the establishment. Mercedes and Cadillacs stand before the door. Nothing in Israel can rival the elegance of the craftsmanship of these huge mansions of prosperous pinkish stone. Those who live here are accustomed to retainers, to chauffeurs and servants, to meals for a score of friends, while their women stay unseen in other quarters. Such luxury comes to them by way of custom, it is a banal confirmation of status and when they see the wife of an Israeli general cooking at her Butagas stove and doing her own baby-sitting, they cannot but triumph in their superiority. Against the social background of the West Bank, Israeli egalitarianism with its practical flavour looks like tasteless thrift.

Among the villas are hotels like the Rabah and the Ramallah-Hilton (which has no connection with other hotels of that name). On certain evenings belly-dancers perform for the clientele, but the girls are Israeli, recruited from Jaffa and Lydda, and they provide their services just as Rafi in the Sinai desert had once anticipated. Whisky, striptease, girly delights, revenge through lubricity – notions of high life cribbed from the West. Not the only importations either, for on this main Ramallah highway is the Frontier Village Society and the shop of Musa Alami's Arab Development Society. The Bible Society too. The Arab Needle-work Shoppe. The Mary Lowell Home for the Blind. The Helen Keller Bible Land Society. The Evangelical Home for Girls, SOS and Caritas. After the squat mosque at Shu'fat is a road-sign, 'Attention! Blinds crossing.' Attention! The Western conscience is at work, doing for the poor and underprivileged what they cannot do for themselves. One charitable promotion after another, and the greatest of these is UNRWA. The Arabs have been encumbered with patronage which they are unable to refuse. Standing in line to receive crumbs and condescension from rich benefactors, they have to despise themselves, but so they extend their demoralization. The hand-outs, like other values of the West, at the same time entice and paralyze: they demarcate rich from poor and reinforce inequalities. The Arabs feel worse because we feel better. The more they got, from a pair of second-hand shoes to statehood, the deeper their guilt and resentment against the giver. Which was their right, and they nurtured it on a timeless inheritance of patience.

Some will never escape such a cast of mind. Mr Bakerjian, for instance, a florid and forceful Armenian, who subjects me for half the morning to a lecture which is *kolubuja* at its most virulent. Nothing good was ever done to or for the Arabs. Unless and until the clock is put back for the refugees to 1947, he says, war in these parts will last till Armageddon. Outside his Area Office an autumn sun lies placid and warm on the town. Workmen in *galibiyehs* are repairing the central circle of the road around a clock which has been mounted as a monument. The usual bustle, passers-by staring, ambling, marketing. Lorries hooting. Beyond the taxi rank is the travel agency of the Mayor of Deir Dibwan. Down the street is the office of Aziz Shehadeh, a tubby and busy lawyer, a Protestant, and one of the brave handful who like his friend Abu Shilbaya have dared in print to call for a Palestinian state and to criticize the Fatah – the Palestinians, he has told me, have always been in the hands of gangsters. Here is the coffee house where I have heard it argued that only a few thousand Jews were really gassed by Hitler. At the hospital with its new kidney machine and blood bank are six devoted nuns, who complain that their patients are so used to sleeping on floors that they will not stay in bed. Dr Salti; the Odeh family, one of whom is a doctor, another a priest who joined the *fedayeen*; Dr Michaels with his big house. The owners of the Sylvana Chocolate Factory have made a fortune, and so have many others like Janho, in league with Sherif Nasser Ben Jamil, the king's uncle, about whom every rumour is rife. Abu Jubran distils his famous *arak* of that name. At Naum's restaurant every day the elite of the West Bank congregate under an espalier of climbing flowers, and dozens of cats fight for scraps around the tables. Ramallah is for the Christians, while adjoining it, El-Bireh is for Moslems and some time ago the boundaries were gerrymandered so that the richer Christians' taxes go to the Moslems. Listen to the verbal sweep of someone like Mr Bakerjian and you would have to believe that the Arabs really exist in only one dimension as passive agents of other people's more vigorous histories, and you would never appreciate that just beyond the window is a life of their own quite as complex, independent and diverting as anyone's.

Aref el-Aref lives in El-Bireh and every visitor to the West Bank must pay him their respects. Eighty now, Aref el-Aref is the fire-eater he always was. During the First World War, as an officer in the Turkish army, he was captured by the Russians at the battle of Erzerum and sent to Siberia. He escaped to join the Arab revolt in the Hejaz under Sherif Hussein and Lawrence, and soon was being a nuisance to the Mandate, which nevertheless he served as a district commissioner. Aref el-Aref has always maintained that he never incited Arabs to kill Jews, but Israelis will produce other evidence. In his house, which has the Turkish atmosphere of its period, he keeps his library. He has been a prolific writer of history, about the Bedouin of Gaza and Beersheba of which towns he has been governor, and about Jerusalem of which he has been mayor. His largest work, *The Tragedy of Palestine*, is in seven volumes. Framed photographs show him in 1921 on a balcony in Jerusalem rousing a mob, for which the British exiled him for a while. On that balcony, he says, he was forecasting the wreckage of Palestine which he now experiences, fifty years on. Day by day he chronicles events in big leatherbound diaries. Informants come to him continually and he writes down what they tell him, supplemented by newspaper cuttings, to provide what is a kind of memorialized grapevine about the occupation, with lists of houses blown up, of dunams expropriated, of people deported. A special volume is devoted to *fedayeen* in prison, and, needless to say, it is a repetition of the claims and confessions given before military courts. Aref el-Aref had a family house near Jerusalem, 'taken in the public interest' as he puts it. The compensation offered was not enough and none of the family touched the money. A photograph of the subsequent ruin is on his desk as a constant reminder. His blue eyes water.

Israelis emerge from his leatherbound books as the purest demons, but he wants a federation with them, and adds that he likes them as people. He returns to his favourite work, *My Dream*, the writing of his youth, and a short romance of a perfected Arab state, nationalistic, lofty, all chains snapped. In its Garibaldian way, this book best imparts the aspirations of Arabs like him to be as they once were, princes, horsemen, before whom infidels quailed. Meanwhile we are brought down to earth by an Israeli telephone engineer out in front who is laying five thousand new lines for the town.

Next time I come to study those leatherbound albums I am early, so call first on Abdul Jawad Salah, the Mayor of El-Bireh, who is reputed to be one of the most independent-minded men on the West Bank. On his door is a studio portrait of Nasser and behind his desk hangs a map in wool of Palestine. The mayor is young, a big man with a manner owing something to his American post-graduate degree. He has been a member of the Arab Nationalist Movement and of the Ba'ath. His ideas, in short, are the up-to-date version of Aref el-Aref's, and the difference in generation is expressed by the mayor's khaki shirt open at the neck, and the almost Israeli way he gets down to business. First he tells me about inexplicable emissaries the Israelis send to him in the guise of journalists. He scribbles a note to his clerk who soon brings back an answer. In fact he has telephoned Aref el-Aref to check that I am really who I claim to be, an Englishman ahead of a midday appointment. Ah, *yanni*, I mean – the mayor punctuates his points. And leaves things unsaid.

Three women have presented themselves in a delegation as the mothers of *fedayeen* held in Ashkelon prison where a scuffle broke out only the day before. It is in the headlines. A warder was slightly hurt. The mothers want permission for a special visit. The mayor telephones the military governor and gets through to a Major Moshe, to whom he spells out in English the names of the three prisoners and the mothers' requests. He gets a promise that he will hear news by the afternoon. It has been an efficient man-to-man talk. I ask about collaboration, and by way of a reply he says that the council had a loan from the Jordanian government, and when repayment became due he refused to let the Israelis collect it. So the council books went without approval. Like Shimon Peres he has his model table of development plans for the town. About six houses have been demolished, one of them belonging to a man who had broken relations with his Fatah son. Deportation alarms him, for the authorities have hinted at it. In his office is also an elderly doctor of the Red Crescent Society whom I had first met some years ago. He had been deported but was now allowed home. *Yanni,* they have promised to be good boys. The Jordanians killed the spirit of the people, that is why it is so quiet.

Aref el-Aref is amused to have been telephoned about my credentials. He has just returned from Amman, from the funeral of a friend. The journey and its implications are too much for him, pushing beyond ideological dead-ends into some open ground of bewilderment where Arabs and Jews are settling down together, where a Major Moshe is on the line to grant permits, where a passionate struggle has no outlet except in scrapbooks. Life is proving more adaptable than this record of it. On the terrace where I leave him, Aref el-Aref sits holding the photograph of the single arch left standing from that family house where he was born.

On the edge of Ramallah is Amari camp. The eye soon learns to spot where refugees live, detecting those conglomerations at once geometric and untidy of one-storey houses, shelters as they have to be called in UNRWA speech, for other words imply permanency. Like Fawwa close to Hebron, Nur Shams at Jenin, or Askar and Balata outside Nablus, Amari has inhabitants well off by local standards, citizens like any other who are working and whose UNRWA rations are not subsistence but a bonus. Nearby is a teachers' training college started in 1962 for over six hundred women, and not far off another for men; bright well-built institutions which put UNRWA beyond criticism for nobody else would have paid that bill. Some refugees in Ramallah took possession of a plot of land belonging to Dr Tannous of Beirut, once a member of the Arab Higher Committee. Real estate values are rising here as everywhere but so far neither the Jordanian nor the Israeli governments have been able to return Dr Tannous his land – the log-jam of insoluble lawsuits and eviction orders is a microcosm of the whole issue.

On the road to Nablus, Jelazoun is past the turn-off to Bethel, past the Jordanian army complex which will be housing the Israeli local administration once it evacuates the Ambassador Hotel. The camp at Jelazoun is creased into the hillside with the innate skill and charm of every village in Palestine. Plenty of water has been laid on in a large pipe which bends down the slope from the road, and the fruit-trees and cypresses grow heavy and fresh against the starkness of the earth. A small central square has shops round it and several *souks* with coffee-houses and television – soon electricity will be available for all. In the first house I enter I am told that the Jews should save themselves the trouble and expense of all this water and electricity by simply packing up the place and sending everyone home.

Like all the camps, Jelazoun has its notables, its *mukhtars*, who boss their quarter. Crucially, they are in charge of seeing how the rations are distributed. UNRWA appoints a camp leader and gives him an office where he can behave as the adjutant he is. A blackboard gives the camp statistics. Before the war, posters exhorted everyone to destroy Israel, but they have been replaced by strip-drawings about hygiene. At Jelazoun in January 1971 the camp leader and five UNRWA employees were arrested for belonging to the Fatah and got sentences ranging from twelve to thirty months. The camp leader's wife, a fat jolly woman with a baby in tow, says that her husband was simply denounced by a refugee with a grudge against him.

Some Israeli sociologists have carried out a unique survey here and found evidence for charges that have often been made: hidden resources, businesses, houses rented out while their owners live in camp, men who are contractors and have several lorries; the sale of ration cards, falsification of deaths and births, and so on – all proofs that the refugees are as others, or perhaps a little more enterprising. Not a survey but a lifetime would be needed to trace the groupings here, the neighbourhood ties, the village origins, the family structures, indicating the admirable tenacity with which these people have done their best to reproduce their former existence. Once they were peasants and now in common with all the refugees they are halfway town-dwellers. Also half the population is under fifteen. A whole generation has grown up ignorant of farming and it is doubtful if they have the skills, let alone the inclination, to return to the land; they are part of the world-wide process of urbanization and industrialization, however slow. They need other qualifications and they acquire them – pride of place on many a wall is given to matriculations and certificates, which are the usual passports to betterment.

Shelters are no longer the concrete blocks once put up by UNRWA; they have been improved. Extra rooms or stairs have been added as often as not, and private latrines installed. Trellises and gardens and vegetable plots abound, the goats or the hens have their corner. Children may race ragged in the streets but in most houses the linen is clean-washed, the bed-blankets neatly spread in the old Arab style, the floors scrubbed. Today at Jelazoun it happens to be Saturday, the Jewish Sabbath, and the men are therefore not working but sitting in their best clothes in the coffee-houses or wandering about, so falling indirectly into the pattern of Israeli life.

The health clinic here has been built by Oxfam opposite the Supplementary Feeding Centre. The personable young doctor was educated in France and Belgium, has a private practice but attends three times a week for UNRWA. He pulls out the files, Infant Health Records, Immunization Records, cards of different colours – the refugees have better health services than the rest of the population. Also better education in scores of UNRWA schools. This is why those who are refugees have been so determined to cling to that status while those who were not have tried every dodge to be classified as such. Registration on the UNRWA rolls is much more than a meal ticket; it is an insurance policy, a promotion, a way of life. Several hundred thousand people who were quite as poor as any refugee managed to infiltrate the rolls and in the 1960s UNRWA, stung by criticism that it was actually swelling the Palestinian problem, tried to weed out the number, without much success. Since the Six-Day War spokesmen no longer bluster on the subject. The Israeli occupation has made it more irrelevant. So a whole lot of Arabs have been receiving goods and services to which they might not have been entitled – who cares? The argument has a sour taste, a little like discussing how many million Jews were actually murdered in the concentration camps.

Kalandia camp is on the way home from Jelazoun and so close to the outskirts of Jerusalem that its northern point, where a few hundred people are housed, has been annexed. The Israelis wanted the nearby airport to be within the city boundaries. On one side of the main road are Jordanian Palestinians who pay no taxes, while across the way are Israeli Palestinians who pay a lot. Over here a motor licence costs practically nothing, over there it is expensive. In 1966 the Jordanian government moved some thousands of these refugees out of the Jewish Quarter of the Old City, which proved a stroke of luck for the Israelis who a year later were to set about restoring the area as it had been. Perhaps some of these lounging young men were the very children who used to chuck stones at sightseers like me at the Wailing Wall during the forbidden time.

Official residents, 500 families; Unofficial, 75; UNRWA, 33; Squatters, 19, declares the Kalandia camp leader's blackboard. A new school has been built, and the kindergarten classes are singing away inside. Trees have been planted, 'so that when the refugees go home we'll have something to remember them by', in the words of an UNRWA man. In the sewing-room women are exquisitely embroidering linen to be sold, and we talk about the *fedayeen* whom the seamstress insists are not terrorists but commandos. The *souk* here has the loudest radios and the grooviest jukeboxes and baby-football tables. Some atmosphere of open-air loud youth has gained the streets over the men in turbans who are sleeping away their old age or prodding at a loaded donkey. The more houses I enter, the more coffee I have to drink until I am worsted by hospitality. Everywhere old-style poverty and new-style gadgetry are bewilderingly mixed. It is lunchtime and the day calms with a hint of advancing siestas. A breeze off the hills greets students descending from the hand-decorated buses with cocks' feathers fluttering on the radiator-cap, a *fantasia* harking back to ancient caravans. In the distance bulldozers are churning, enlarging the airport runway and laying the foundations of a complex of science-based industries. Soon Kalandia will be as much part of modern Jerusalem as Ramat Eshkol, French Hill and Nebi Samwil.

On the West Bank Aqabat Jaber is the only camp with a difference. In the Jordan valley between Jericho and the Allenby Bridge, it is close by Musa Alami's farms of the Arab Development Society. I go down there with the camp leader Ibrahim Abu Rish in his white Mercedes, and with us comes his brother Mahmud, the Mayor of El-Azzariya, or Bethany to Christians. Ibrahim has a high complexion and both brothers look like men who get what they want. Ibrahim started the refugee camp across the river at Karameh, and moved to Aqabat Jaber in 1952 when it was still tented. At the same time the brothers helped to construct a new village called Mansour, a resettlement which would have been quite impossible had they not been important local notables (as described fondly by Stewart Perowne in his book *The One Remains*).

An avenue of flame trees, of bensianas, vivid with red flowers, leads into the camp. A big interior wall was built by boys at a training school. The office is the normal hut, roofed with sack lining, and it has photographs of President Kennedy and of such occasions as the visit of an American basketball team. Above the door an inscription from the Koran explains the duty of kindness to strangers.

In this largest of Palestinian camps there were 60,000 refugees of whom about 5,000 remain. On the Wednesday of the Six-Day War, the place was abandoned in a stampede which could be heard in Jericho, or so people like to claim. The flight was infectious, as a dancing frenzy might have been. Aqabat Jaber was always a turbulent place, open to demagogues, and several times the Jordanian authorities had to call out troops to control it, and even fire on the mob. Curfews, trials, executions – another Abu Rish brother had been hanged when Suleiman Nabulsi was Prime Minister of Jordan.

The camp leaders, the UNRWA officials and their assistants, Saleh Abdo, the owner of the Hisham Palace Hotel and Mayor of Jericho (his predecessor having been deported, and Fawzi Arakat before him having fled on the Tuesday of the war), Redwan el-Hilou who is former secretary of the Palestine Communist Party and an old Jericho veteran if ever there was one, they all say the same about that stampede: the people of Aqabat Jaber realized that the Jordanian army had been destroyed under their eyes, they were afraid that the Jews would kill them, or at least deprive them of rations and refugee cards. With his wife and children, Ibrahim stood at the camp entrance by the flame trees to demonstrate that his family would be sharing the common lot. Nobody was in a mood for such examples.

Improvised in adobe bricks, the houses are no longer maintained and will soon entirely crumble away – earth to earth. Families used to live in compounds, piled together higgledy-piggledy in a Central or South American style. Blackened streaks on walls are the only signs of any kitchen. Any conceivable thing like bamboo, poles, corrugated iron, had been poked into roofing or into extra angular bits and pieces, a lot of it now looted or missing. Not so much as an old shoe has been discarded. On floor after floor the contours of faeces, sunbaked and imperturbable in the decay, are all that is left of human habitation. In the past, the summer heat made the smell unbearable and a grant from Switzerland was spent installing private latrines in every house. In this climate dysentery can kill babies and they have to be treated in a special Dehydration Centre in the clinic. There is also a Malaria Section. One of the four schools is still open and in the circumstances it has to be coeducational for its four hundred pupils. The children are in tidy green-stripey smocks. Maps of Palestine hang on the walls. The headmistress is capable, and in her room is a wonderfully ornate blackboard drawing in multi-coloured chalks of the classroom numbers – a symbol somehow of the perpetual losing struggle to preserve order amid encroaching chaos.

By the school fence a mad woman is shouting at the sky. A second, younger, mad woman grins through the window of the white Mercedes. She has a few things to get off her chest to Ibrahim but hardly has time before a companion comes up, a stout lady in flowing robes with a tray-load of *pitta* balanced on her head. At each sentence of the mad woman, her friend punches her on the jaw with an extraordinary blend of firmness and delicacy which takes into account everybody's feelings. The insane, the infirm, the old, those who have been rejected, they are squatting in the feeding centre. 'Dirty thieving bastards from Gaza' we are told about a small knot of families apparently living out of doors, as shapes here and there in the precious shade. Dust everywhere – the interior of the car is powdered with it. In the *souk* are a few shops, one of them calling itself the Modern Butchery. At last a house appears inhabited, and in it stands a fine straight-backed and smiling young woman. She moved in when the others fled and has a whole compound to herself. Her baby swings asleep in a cradle cobbled from scrap-iron while flies gather groggily on its mosquito net. She lifts this net to wipe sweat off the child's forehead. A pair of underpants which are out to dry have been run up from a US Aid flour bag. Her husband is earning the equivalent of four dollars a day or four times what he had before the war. She is raising ducks and hens, she prepares food, she shows us what self-evidently we have to see as her good fortune, under the simple and ancient magic of the Hand of Fatima – which is no other than her own left-hand dipped into blue dye and stamped on every available surface, a brilliant mark for fertility and this continuing luck.

Ibrahim has to telephone the Military Governor of Jericho about a man who is sick and cannot keep an appointment the following day to collect a permit to Amman. Back in his hut under a lazily swinging fan he asks for Itzig, and Sieber, and complains that they cannot speak Arabic, or English, come to that. Mahmud leaves with me, to drive a kilometre or two to Nu'ami, an extension of Aqabat Jaber but empty and reduced to straight lines of nothingness – a ghost town, with beyond its fallen wire perimeter the joking voices of American tourists who have come for snapshots of each other in King Hisham's Palace with its broken columns and stone tracery. Rich hot scents waft over from the thick-leafed banana plantations. Another kilo-metre, and at Ein-es-Sultan another patchwork of abandoned refugee houses rises on low foothills. In this stale squalor, and on a corner of its own, is a mysteriously splendid stone house with a curving wing and smart green ironwork and shutters. At its entrance a lone guardian lolls on a bedding-roll, knitting with spectacles at a tilt on his nose. A dog leaps out barking. A cen-tury or so rolls away as I seem to be standing in some mid-Victorian lithograph come to life, of the Middle East as Euro-peans then saw it, with Arabs as nomads perched poetically but inexplicably in a landscape pitiless enough to wreck each successive age.

Home again, Mahmud invites me to eat in the house of a neighbour who had been an officer in King Hussein's bodyguard until he took part in the ill-fated coup after Suleiman Nabulsi's period in office, more for the fun of the thing, as he describes it, than out of expectation of power. Like so many Palestinians, he did his time in the desert prison at Jafr and there, to clean his kit, he paid a batman who later became a leader of the Fatah. It was beyond his imagining that a former prison orderly should have offered him, a Sandhurst-trained officer, a post with the *fedayeen*. Proudly he shows his records of the good old days, when he cut a figure on ceremonial duties, sword drawn – until Mahmud invites me to his own house at El-Azzariya.

The car just has space up a sharply stony track between walls of blinding whiteness, between the convents and churches in honour of the village's most enduring celebrities, Martha and Mary and Lazarus. Halfway is a Moslem cemetery where men and their sons have been at someone's burial. At the top the view encompasses the hills towards the Dead Sea. In Mahmud's cool and spacious house is a mint copy of Stewart Perowne's book with its photographs of the Abu Rishes, as well as several highly polished brass shell-cases, the biggest of them a British six-pounder, mementoes of 1948 when a man might still face his enemy and fight as his forefathers had, before the superpowers had converted the human element into another of their world-wide weapons systems. During the Six-Day War, Mahmud says, two hundred villagers sheltered in his cellars. They were terrified, they had to be restrained from running to Amman. On the Friday evening of that week a boy arrived with the news that the Jews were waiting down the road with a column of tanks. Everyone in the house gave Mahmud up for dead. Actually what the Jews wanted was a billet for the night and they were offered the fourteen rooms of the boys' school. But the janitor had run away, taking the key with him. 'You see,' Mahmud tells the story with a reflective air, 'what the issue came down to between Jews and Arabs was who should break the lock off the door.'

As a travel book *Eothen* has a surviving warmth and perception. Kinglake's account from the 1840s of one of the principal towns of Palestine reaches to the present.

Nablus is the very furnace of Mahometan bigotry; and I believe that only a few months before the time of my going there, it would have been madly rash for a man, unless strongly guarded, to show himself to the people of the town in a Frank costume; but since their last insurrection, the Mahometans of the place had been so far subdued by the severity of Ibrahim Pasha, that they dared not now offer the slightest insult to a European. It was quite plain, however, that the effect with which the men of the old school refrained from expressing their opinion of a hat and a coat was horribly painful to them. As I walked through the streets and bazaars, a dead silence prevailed. Every man suspended his employment, and gazed on me with a fixed glassy look, which seemed to say, 'God is good: but how marvellous and inscrutable are His ways that thus He permits this white-faced dog of a Christian to hunt through the paths of the faithful!'

A decade or so later, another English observer was Mary Rogers, wife of the first British consul in Jerusalem. Her *Domestic Life in Palestine* is a record not only of the tiny

Anglican community growing round Bishop Gobat and his new church school but also of the Turkish world of *kavass* and *bimbachis*. Dedicated to Holman Hunt, 'In remembrance of the pleasant visits which I paid to his studio on Mount Zion', the book has a pre-Raphaelite concern with detail which was to vanish in the approaching age of nationalism. To most Westerners Arab society has looked either touchingly elemental or else treacherously deep, and sometimes both simultaneously, which has prompted much moralizing. Not from Mrs Rogers though, Victorian lady that she was. In Nablus she found four main factions, two of them being the Abdul Hadis and the Tuqans. Recently Touad Abdul Hadi was sent to prison with Randa Nabulsi and her sister (themselves the nieces of ex-Prime Minister Suleiman Nabulsi) for sabotage on behalf of the PFLP. She is out now and teaching in school again. Hazem Abdul Hadi is a bookseller and journalist in Jenin, as well as being the son of the previous mayor. Dr Kadri Tuqan is no more, alas, and behind his funeral cortège walked a crowd of thousands, among them the Military Governor of Nablus and his advisers. At the very heart of Nablus is still the *sabenah* or parliament of the Tuqans, a vaulted medieval building just as Mrs Rogers saw it, and where the family business of making olive oil and soap is carried on. In the dark basements cauldrons bubble, while upstairs, the finished bars are stacked in a white lattice-work of rising circles.

The oils and soaps of Nablus are famous throughout the Arab world and have made the fortune of several other factory-owners, of the ex-Mayor Hamdi Cana'an, and of Walid Shaqah whose father Ahmed was one of the richest men on the West Bank. The el-Masri family have a flour mill as well – Haj Maz'uz el-Masri is the present mayor; his cousin Hikmet el-Masri is the biggest businessman in town and in the Jordanian Senate until lately; Wasfi el-Masri has been a senior member of the Jordanian Bar. Abdul Latif Anabtawi is the head of another prominent family and a present member of the Senate.

The right to vote in Jordan, and therefore on the West Bank, depends upon a property qualification. Money and politics are therefore unusually tightly welded together in a way which tends to arouse scorn on the part of Israelis and younger more radical Arabs alike. Rare are those who amass money without regard to political influences, although some do, like the Alluls who are merchants, or Hevzi Malhis who started a plastic shoe factory after the war. The Suchtians, returning from Houston, Texas, have opened a drug-pharmacy business. Abu Hashem, once a peasant, has been steadily acquiring land in the Jordan valley and now has constructed for himself the largest house in Nablus.

Several men among what is known as the traditional leadership owe the start of their careers to the Mandate administration which helped to strengthen them in their positions. They have become connected by marriage. Hamdi Cana'an and Hikmet el-Masri have married Shaqah sisters, though of different mothers. (Hamdi's son in fact has broken away and is a lecturer in the American University of Beirut.) More to the point, these traditional leaders have the ear of the king and his government across the river and of the Israelis over the hills. Together with Sheikh Ali Ja'abari and the handful of Jerusalemites, they can make of West Bank opinion more or less what they like. Their comings and goings, either privately or in delegations to Amman or Beirut or Cairo to argue the West Bank case about such matters as a projected Arab boycott of their goods, are political events and reported as such. In 1968, for instance, some of these notables approached the Israelis with a plan to restore Arab civilian administration on the West Bank, and to elect one among them as an Arab governor. In a broadcast from Amman Bahjat Talhouni, Jordanian prime minister at the time, spoke about 'this imperialist and Zionist design' and backed up his criticism with more subsidies of money and threatening letters. The idea was dropped. Traffic on the Allenby Bridge, after all, is two-way.

On the assumption that one day a reception committee might be standing on some flag-bedecked platform to welcome back King Hussein into his proposed United Arab Kingdom, the Nablus establishment has to keep a constant weather-eye on

Amman and be as wary as it knows how. Neither Jordan nor Israel would willingly take a step which might disaffect the West Bank – that is the factor opening up several power-plays. To be courted by rivals who are for the moment in a stand-off has brought greater local independence. For reasons of internal security the Israeli authorities have muzzled the opposition of Communists and militant Ba'athists. None of the traditional leadership can have been sorry when the Israelis expelled to Amman communists like Dr Dallal, Adnan Bakry or Rushdi Shahin, the latter having lived underground in the town for several years while the Jordanian police had been after him. Not since the Mandate has the traditional leadership been put so firmly in the saddle. There is nobody to replace them. No wonder, then, that Fatah tried to make the Nablus *casbah* its headquarters, in the hopes of cashing in on social as well as political discontent. No wonder, either, that as in Kinglake's day men of the old school refrain from expressing their opinions. Once this was illustrated for me in a coffee-house when talk was brought to a stop by the entry of a man who happened to be a cousin of Mohamed Rasoul, the head of the Jordanian security services away in Amman. If prudence is a virtue which will be rewarded, imprudence may carry a death sentence.

During the two or three years immediately after the war, a walk in the streets and bazaars of Nablus was an uncomfortable experience. People did suspend their employment and that fixed glassy look had plainly survived the generations from Ibrahim Pasha to the Israelis. The most determined strikes and protest demonstrations had been organized by teachers. The Women's Association has been very active, not only on account of its experienced leader Andalib el-Awwad, but also because its members include the daughters of the powerful families (which prompts Israeli sociologists into musings about the role of women in Arab society).

As mayor, Hamdi Cana'an had proved unable to sustain the hopeless task of riding turbulence and appeasing the Israelis. More than once his resignation was offered, if reluctantly, but its final acceptance in March 1969 was probably unavoidable.

A few weeks beforehand, the *fedayeen* had scored one of their big successes when a patrol holed up in a cave and in the subsequent shoot-out killed Colonel Ofer, who was directing operations against them, having been previously the Military Governor of Nablus.

The succeeding military governor, Shaul Givoli, has the reputation again of 'a perfect gentleman' and he is so described by men who are often caricatures of the British on whom they have so visibly modelled themselves, down to pinstripe worsted suits, discreet ties and a golf-club moustache. To judge by the grapevine, Colonel Givoli has put himself out to be accessible, to have treated each issue personally in order to be responsible for whatever happens. (*Maariv*, the evening paper, publishes his historical fiction under the by-line S. Givoli, Nablus.) One may now stroll to the new Gamel Abdul Nasser Memorial Park – which would not be laid out in Amman – to the Commercial Centre of the el-Masris, to the Chamber of Commerce with its Gothic-English lettering above the door, or into the meanest and crookedest part of the *casbah*, and attract no attention, no more fixed glassy looks. No dead silence. The Arab policeman with an Israeli badge pinned to his Jordanian uniform directs traffic from his little kiosk as he always has. *Chic Bébé* stocks European fashions. Arab and Israeli commodities or newspapers are displayed in the shop-windows. Israeli signs for garages or licensed agencies or for the office of the Custodian of Absentee Property are not defaced. Children on the wing may shriek insults about dirty Jews, but a shout back at them in the same idiom and they will smile and scamper. In the middle of 1971 three grenades were rolled harmlessly along the main street and the joke spread that someone had been paid by the *fedayeen* to throw them and by the Israelis to keep the pins in.

At the town's entrance, just beyond the milestone indicating Jacob's Well, stands the prison. At visiting times whole families together press to the entrance. Next door is the Taggart building used by the military governor. A few hundred yards farther on is the new Municipality, and beyond it some open space where buses are parked around lots of scrap and refuse and junked car-bodies, leading to the central square with the Tuqan *sabenah*. The layout itself suggests how best, how swiftly, the mob from the *casbah* should mobilize and be channelled straight along to Haj Maz'uz el-Masri in the Municipality or on to Colonel Givoli – which is the eventuality Israeli policy is designed to prevent, forestalling that fatal moment when it is too late and tear-gas canisters, or worse, live ammunition, have to be issued from the stores.

At the end of the summer, that attack on the warder in Ashkelon prison was a typical pretext for the trouble which might be tapped just under the surface. If mothers in El-Bireh could organize and call on their mayor, so could the women of Nablus. I learnt about a planned protest from an anonymous message left in my hotel by friends from Nablus, but the Israelis knew in any case for one of them also rang me up to say that it would be instructive to attend. In the morning about forty ladies from the families of the traditional leadership or the upper class sat in corridors and rooms at the Municipality, and then went with Haj Maz'uz to hand a petition to Shaul Givoli. Orders came from above that such demonstrations would effectively put a stop to any prison visiting. Meanwhile a protest had been made, which was worth a paragraph in the Western papers; Nablus had gone about its business, the peace had been kept, honour was satisfied.

A necessary ritual, it might be supposed, like so many happenings of this kind across the world, but actually it calls into question the whole nature of hatred, or that furnace of bigotry in Kinglake's terms, which everyone had been led to expect. It has been axiomatic that the Arabs hate the Israelis. Every Israeli administrator will acknowledge as much when he drops his favourite cliché that he does not expect to be loved by the Arabs. You look at Nablus, so reputed for its special hatred, at the new green-domed mosque built by the el-Masris as a condition for being granted the land surrounding it. You go to the comfortable villas of the Rafidiya and Ashrafiya districts, to sit in rooms which have a late, late echo of the heaviest

French taste. You consult the radical-chic set like Remonda Tawil originally from a Christian Arab family near Acre before she left Israel in 1957 and who used to write 'A Letter from Nablus' for Abu Zuluf's old newspaper, and her friends Dr Kilani of UNRWA, and Nihaia, one of the several daughters of Hikmet el-Masri and married to another doctor. You interview Hida el-Khayet, of quite a well-known family, herself a dentist's assistant and avowed *fedayeen* sympathizer.

Fadwa Tuqan is the younger sister of Ahmed Tuqan, head of the family and briefly Prime Minister in Jordan before the Six-Day War. A poet, she is among the best-known of Arab intellectuals, a petite woman with a precise soft voice and expressive eyes. She has been to Russia and China. She calls herself a nationalist and a socialist. In Nablus during the war, she says, she was sure that the Arabs would win, that the day of liberation was at hand. For a month afterwards she could not bring herself to go down into the town, for a sight of the little white flags everywhere, and of the Jews – and her eyes fill with tears as she speaks. A poem called 'The Plague' did justice to her emotions. She gave readings on the West Bank, including the publicized passage about her desire to eat the livers of Jews. The military governor asked her how she could say a thing like that, General Dayan took an interest and arranged for Hamdi Cana'an to drive her over to his house at Zahala. 'You hate us,' were his opening words. True, for were they not hateful, putting her friend Randa Nabulsi into prison, and should she not have believed that the *fedayeen* were larger than life? 'You're right,' she quotes Dayan, 'but what's the use?' There is no answer, in Fadwa Tuqan's house or in Dayan's house, or anywhere, but of the telling of stories there is no end. A Tuqan cousin of hers, she says, had two Jewish wives, one of whom lives in Tel Aviv and has sons in Saudi Arabia. At the bridge this summer, the Jewish mother had a first meeting with her Arab sons in twenty years, and then had to part with them again.

Once, when I am sitting in Remonda Tawil's house nearby,

Fadwa Tuqan sends over a translation she has made from Bialik, of all poets.

> This is nothing else, save that many a time
> you have afflicted us,
> If into beasts of prey you have turned us
> And with cruel wrath
> Your blood we shall drink, and
> We shall not pity you
> As all the people awoke and arose
> And said : revenge!

Almost everybody finds on the West Bank whatever he came to find, and no doubt there are some who would consider this poem to be a cherishing of hatred, but it is not, any more than the prison protest was. Primitive as hatred is, it must have an outlet, it must be able to cope with the voice asking, 'What's the use?' With no outlet, hatred is impotent, it dribbles away into self-hatred or else grows into a form of curiosity about the enemy who can arouse such feelings in us. And that in turn engenders self-pity and admiration, even love, for that enemy.

No matter from what direction it comes, the West Bankers need release. 'We are not Red Indians.' Hikmet el-Masri is the first to make the analogy to me but it was doing the rounds as far as Beirut and Amman. In other words they must assert themselves, break out of *kolubuja*, and project stronger images to live up to, of revenge-seeking beasts and blood-drinkers. Exactly as those in prison convert their plight into heroism. Arabs are as quick to quarrel as anybody but they are not malicious, they have generous reconciliations, the *sulha*, and through this time-honoured custom even hatred becomes an expedient, like friendship. Proper hatred of the Israelis would be so much easier than this slippery and unwilling slide into toleration. The harder reality is forcing reconciliation on them and turning everything into expedience, the more the big words and *kolubuja* images protect the mind. Hence the impact of pathos in a poem like this – it is a plea for integrity.

An outside inquirer becomes familiar with quite a rigid cultural pattern. West Bank activists will begin by denouncing

the Jews and all their works: they will elaborate this into
recriminations of the Arabs for being so abject, blaming themselves exaggeratedly for their own faults and showing up
everybody's behaviour in the worst light – after which you are
a friend, you may drop in whenever you please and treat
their house as yours. So it ceases to be a surprise that someone
who is on public record as wanting the death of every Jew in
fact spends weekends at a kibbutz; or that someone else who is
proud of Fatah connections takes loans from the Israelis; or that
the rich and radical-chic Nabulsis set off in their Mercedes for
good times and shopping sprees in Tel Aviv. Nobody is so
extreme that he is not flattered to have Shaul Givoli and his staff
to a meal which has to be prepared all day. In Nablus, finally, a
gentleman's agreement has been reached between Arab lawyers
and the Israeli prosecutor not to read out in military courts any
confessions dealt with in a petty case. The public no longer
knows what was or was not said during a prisoner's interrogation. Each prisoner is thereby spared the need to come up with
torture stories to justify himself, and save face before his family
and friends. And indeed, since this agreement was put into
practice early in 1970, there has been no more talk of torture.

Climbing geraniums, freesias, hibiscus. Plumbago in bundles
of blue on dressed stone walls. The terraces look spell-bound in
the clear sun. Nablus is pretty, it is close, on a scale of intimacy.
Go and call on Yusuf Ridha, the UNRWA representative for
Samaria, or drive out to Taluza, the beautiful village of Abdel
Rauf Faris, once a Jordanian deputy, and somehow the gossip
has preceded you. Above Ashrafiya, above the trim dome of St
Luke's next to which a superannuated British consul used to live,
is Hamdi Cana'an's house. There too is Walid Shaqah (getting
into his big chauffeur-driven Buick on his way, as everybody
appears already to know that morning, to lunch in Jerusalem
with Musa Alami). A couple of terriers frisk in the gravel circle
of Hamdi Cana'an's garden. An Italian architect was specially
commissioned to design this place. Marble flagging, potted
palms, high-backed chairs as large as thrones; a miraculous hard-
coloured view. No Israeli lives so well. At last I can put my

question about the town clerk who was supposedly hung up by the wrists. Well, perhaps not – but he was in a tiny cell. We have both been round Nablus prison and know that it has no such tiny cell. No indeed, but perhaps there is one somewhere else, and why bring this up anyhow, because the excellent Captain Golan has been transferred to Beersheba, the town clerk is back at work with the Municipality, and nothing bad has happened for well over a year.

We settle down to the comforts of politics. Since the Jordanian civil war, Hamdi Cana'an has changed his mind, and, occupation or no, he wants elections. The el-Masris do not, but Hamdi is confident (wrongly, as it happens) that he will get the better of this round of personal and local jockeying, and end up once more in the mayor's office. The Military Government will allow no boycotting when the Arabs vote for the Municipal Councils for the first time in nine years. Representation within their community is an Arab affair and not to be treated as an anti-Israeli political device. After some dallying Amman has come round to this view too, holding that it is wiser to support well-tried old-timers than denounce the whole operation and run the risk of new or appointed men who might get up to anything with the Israelis. The Israelis must then withdraw for the Palestinians and the king to settle things between them. Partial autonomy, federation – the king has plans. We steer through the thickets of his relationships with King Hussein, with Bahjat Talhouni, Wasfi Tel and General Dayan; all the old foxes, to use the Arab expression. Somewhere behind these speculations can be sensed the mob whose feet may yet be set drumming on the Nablus cobbles, given the right cues and catch-words.

Down at the Tuqan *sabenah* the prospects for the elections can be checked. The news of the moment too. Dr Sami Taktak, from a well-known Christian family, has resigned as director of Nablus Hospital. General Vardi, the Military Governor of the West Bank, and known to some as Vardi Pasha, has paid a flying visit to the town. In no time the grapevine is busy – Dr Taktak is thought to have been intolerably criticized, the Israelis are accused of withholding medicines and facilities. Rows, prejudices, high political colouring. In fact the Jordanians did finish but not equip a new military hospital here and the Israelis have done nothing with its shell. Just before the war Dr Taktak's old General Hospital had seven doctors paid by the Jordanian government. In order to stop these doctors carrying on a lucrative private practice, the Jordanian government had almost doubled their salaries on condition that they then worked solely for the hospital as specified in their contracts. Since the occupation, however, the doctors had again started illegal surgeries at home, once more doubling up their incomes, which might amount to thirty thousand dollars, tax free. One afternoon the Israeli medical inspector, a Dr Pridan, had arrived at the hospital and found no doctor on duty. So he had called round at someone's house and found the man operating on a patient. Instead of reporting him, Dr Pridan had apparently just issued a caution. Therefore Dr Pridan was popularly assumed in Nablus to be in the pay of the doctors, and therefore Vardi Pasha had been speeding along in his black car, and therefore Dr Taktak had resigned.

Over the days the story unravels, but always·has one more perspective. I chase about in the Israeli administration in the Ambassador Hotel. The guards fumble with chits. By now most of the departments in this shambling place are familiar, with their dingy passages and disused bathrooms piled high with the usual bumf out of which civil servants construct their nests like a species of faithful bird. Each time I seem to leave the hotel with another armful of printed material in which the statistics of consumption and production are always rising. On the walls are photographs mounted on boards of the West Bankers as the Israelis would like to see them, as progressive farmers still in their *keffiyehs* but climbing on to shiny tractors or exulting over improved tomatoes, as roadlayers, drainers and surveyors and nurses, as women and children picturesquely and immemorially using an olive press or threshing corn by hand.

The head of the medical department for the West Bank is Dr Kafka from Prague, where he had a famous cousin. He wants to tell me about new mobile clinics for villages and not about the Nablus doctors. He defends them. The door opens and poor Dr Pridan pops his head round. '*Sie brauchen mir nicht?*' They make an appointment for me to talk to Dr Taktak's successor, Dr Fayek el-Masri.

The Nablus hospital, like the prison, was put up by the Turks. On his first day there Dr el-Masri takes me round. His white coat has a red name-tape, Dr Taktak's, stitched on the collar. Council members, one of them a Tuqan, are kept waiting. So is Soleiman Nabulsi's brother, the father of Randa, and one of whose grandchildren is in hospital. The huge high-ceilinged rooms have fine Ottoman decorations, but they are packed out. A patient is attended by most of his family. Children run everywhere, the old stare blankly: human life is at its most eager and wretched as in some illustration, say of Scutari before Florence Nightingale took charge. Dr el-Masri, a member of the family and married to another daughter of Hikmet's, has been trained in America where he ran a hospital department. He made arrangements to keep his private practice, which he says earns him one of the largest salaries on the West Bank. As for the other doctors, their clinics were clandestine, their actions were detrimental, they were profiteers. The government, whether Israeli or Jordanian, should insist on its contractual rights. This whole building, however, must be demolished. Why, the desk at which he sits was the one at which he passed his viva in 1946 before a British panel.

Friends in the town are also doctors with private practices. We have a noisy lunch during which it is argued by the Arabs present that this scandalous hospital to-do once more proves them to be irredeemably corrupt, that the traditional leadership has a stranglehold which only the Israelis can break. Nablus hospital should be as good as Hadassah and the Israelis must see to it. In effect, the Israelis should radicalize the Arabs for them. Otherwise the Arabs really will turn into Red Indians. The Israelis must give everyone the vote, women included, and then order elections; they must sweep away the reactionary past.

But should Israelis really have any such responsibility for Arabs? And if they have, by historical accident, should not this responsibility be to leave the Arabs alone, exactly as they found them? To tamper with another society, let alone to remake it with different values, would be what is meant by colonialism. And yet that is what modernists on the West Bank advocate, though perhaps they lean on the knowledge that traditional Zionists want nothing to do with them. Progressive, reactionary? Labels do not fit a riddle like this.

General Gazit has the title of Coordinator of the Occupied Territories. He is responsible to General Dayan, and his office is in Ha-Kiryat, the Tel Aviv Ministry of Defence. The elevator does not stop on his floor – it is like trying to find one's way in some swollen American campus. And whom should they deal with except the traditional leadership, General Gazit wants to know, there is nobody else, the so-called professional classes and radicals have no following. Then why should some of them have been deported? As far as the general is concerned, an Arab can hold whatever opinions he likes, he can intrigue with his friends so long as he does not provoke a riot – violence must be nipped long before it buds. The telephone rings, and it is General Vardi with the latest news of the round-up of a network of about a hundred men in Hebron. They had actually done no act of sabotage, which means that they must have been denounced. Give it another six months, the general says, and probably others will have organized again. He pushes at the black frame of his spectacles; he has the air of tired severity which top Israeli officials like to cultivate, and he talks as he has talked a thousand times before: the *fedayeen* had a nuisance value, but now they and the West Bank and the Gaza Strip are simply a function of what happens on the Suez Canal. If there is an interim solution with Egypt on the canal, then there can be one on the West Bank. Otherwise not. Meanwhile it is like running a bath, one tap is hot, the other is cold, and you turn them to suit yourself, it being of no importance which is which. All the time the economy is being developed into something self-sustaining, the necessary infrastructure is taking shape. Life is normal. More sophistication, more quiet pessimism, and the tutorial is ended.

I just have time to ask him to sanction a meeting with Shaul Givoli. Speak to General Vardi, he advises, and so I do, at the end of the week, in the Military Headquarters in Jerusalem. Vardi takes his time (he would like me to explain the kind of books I write) while a secretary serves cakes and coffee. His expressionless administrator's face gives away nothing, but he is unexpectedly frank. He answers each question fully, and delves into it with the facts and figures tidily marshalled. Three years ago he used to think that the Nablus demonstrators who carried banners, 'We are all Fatah', would be crossing the river to make for the nearest recruiting office. But they did not. Words were not translated into deeds, and the population has less sympathy for the *fedayeen* than before. Maoist theory has been tested and found wanting. Occupation is a matter of threats. The policy of demolishing houses had succeeded because it had obviated the use of even harsher methods. To establish security was to give the Arabs freedom to operate civil affairs, and this benefit to the whole population itself contributed to security, thus completing a circle. Infrastructure again – the word is clearly the order of the day.

The next step is the demand for political representation, as in these municipal elections. The moment will come, Vardi thinks, when the Palestinians will decide to speak directly to the Israelis, when I shall be able to write about the part played by direct contact between Arabs and Jews – and the general smacks the table hard. Should both parties desire it at that point, there will be a Palestine state. Until then, the Israelis cannot grant what the West Bankers do not demand.

General Vardi has served in the Far East, and knows about corruption. As in the case of Nablus Hospital, the population is conditioned to it and makes no formal complaint. The labour exchange director at Ramallah has been arrested for graft. But what would I have him do? Start a witch-hunt and pull everybody into prison? On what basis? He too has to decide what to believe but at least he is willing to act on hard information.

In the end he authorizes me to meet not Shaul Givoli but Colonel Feldman, Military Governor of Ramallah and the 'perfect gentleman' of Musa Alami's television interview. In the Ramallah Compound, Colonel Feldman and I sit in a room just a few doors away from the court where I have listened to Antun Jaser. A governor has to know everything in his area – Colonel Feldman states a principle and goes on to describe its practice, the personalities like Abdul Jawad Salah of El-Bireh, and Aref el-Aref who once also held this same governorship. He has brought in an Israeli manager to advise on hotels, on improvements for tourists. Previously Governor of Jericho, he likes straight talk from the Arabs and gets irritated only if they go behind his back. Notables ring up and make appointments with him but for one fixed day a week he walks round town and makes himself available to one and all, like a caliph of classical Arabia. As a soldier, he carries a gun. And besides, he likes his wife and children to be with him when convenient. Another day in the week he spends visiting villages. Sometimes he tells the *mukhtars* he is coming, sometimes he just drops by.

A special officer collects applications, reads them, and then decides what to do. His own superiors determine policy, of course, but he can push. So far he has granted some 2,500 family reunification permits and these demand a lot of administrative energy. That morning a prominent merchant had come to his office with special requests for seven reunification permits. Colonel Feldman had been particularly annoyed, for he knew that this man was acting as a *wasta* or go-between, and would be paid for the service, quite unnecessarily, by each family. The seven families had only to apply directly and he would sign, as was his duty. So the merchant should not have been trying this fiddle, he had been unceremoniously thrown out and the seven families had been summoned to the office to fetch their signed permits in person. And certainly that merchant becomes the personal enemy of Colonel Feldman and will have to recover face somehow in the future. In this incident are summarized differences which cannot be bridged between the Israeli bureaucratic approach and the Arab personal deal. The two societies do business on standards arising out of cultures and histories which have so little in common. But if there is much more of this occupation, one or the other will have to make accommodations. A secretary interrupts and Colonel Feldman looks a bit embarrassed: acting on a tip-off, he has to sign then and there an order for the arrest of some suspected *fedayeen* in one of the villages.

A tempo of quickening bafflement, the wish to be rid of the whole thing and to be appreciated as well – the emotional attitudes of the Israeli administration on the West Bank are immediately communicated, and they rub off too. Israeli drivers, for instance, do not stop for Israeli women crossing the road, on the contrary they hoot and press forward, but for Arab women they slow down and wait. Imitating this, as you soon are doing, you are condescending to somebody – but to whom? General Vardi and Colonel Feldman and no doubt Shaul Givoli and the rest of them confess that they lose hope but the next day they recover because there is no alternative, because the Arabs are queueing at their door, the family reunification permits have to be signed, or the new nursery school opened, or a religious festival observed and a feast eaten.

You join the procession hastening round and round the West Bank, you sound opinion and check it, you become knotted into the multiple aspects of everything. You take days off to explore mountain villages as remotely and peacefully drowsy as ever, where the *mukhtar* offers a meal of a lavishness which you guiltily wonder if he can afford, and you spend the hours afterwards swopping wisdoms about Sitna Mariam, the Virgin Mary, or Mecca and Islam. You go to Halhul which the Israelis were once accused of razing and you find a prosperous place spreading on dollars from its expatriate sons in America, and where the men in the coffee-houses laugh at themselves for having run away in the war – those with wings should fly, the Jordanian governor had said. In Hebron Sheikh Ali Ja'abari is shrewd and majestic and, ask him whatever ingenious questions you can, you will still get rhetorically evasive answers. Peace – and he leans back at his desk for the utterance – is as far away as the moon. The Jews have returned to Hebron, true, but how many more dunams must they expropriate? He presses his fingers deliberately over his eyelids. His turban appears a great weight. The wisest old fox of them all. His Eminence perfectly well remembers other visits, as well as the bad manners and foolishness of the journalists at his press conference after the war. And he appraises you till you feel ashamed at obtruding with trivial matters about Jews and Arabs and who did what to whom.

More of this and you realize that where hatred has evaporated an almost morbid sentimentality may replace it. An Israeli senior political officer on the West Bank takes this parable from real life: an Arab friend comes to him to tell the story of a dream he had in which the two of them had met by chance in a foreign country and decided to behave as they would have done at home; they ate together, but they were observed so that on returning to the West Bank the Arab found himself arrested by Arab police for fraternizing with the enemy. Just as the judge was summing up the case he awoke and was sorry because now he would not know what sentence his subconscious would pass on him for collaboration.

But of course the Israelis can be held to their names: they are Major Moshe, Itzig, Sieber, Colonel Feldman and General Gazit, Dr Kafka and Dr Pridan, and their photographs appear in the newspapers with good news or bad, while the Arabs, with the exceptions of the few traditional leaders, are not recorded by anything much more public than the mark their fathers may have left before them. What could Kinglake note except a fixed glassy look? The *fellah* walks across a plough-scratched field, his wife and children in their loose clothes are behind, or squatting by the twisty roadside and tending goats: representative figures. The Unknown Arab. The traffic, the occupation passes them by. These people look you through, through the rocks.

Their lives appear so simple that you should be able to look through them but you cannot. They cannot be possessed by strangers, nor dispossessed, as if they are not quite there, yet more there than anyone else.

7 · The Lion's Carcass

And Samson said,
Let me die with the Philistines.

Towards the Gaza Strip the countryside thins as if no longer bothering to try. The fields peter into sand, the stumpy relics of British army camps are frequent and dispiriting. Cotton is grown and at its harvesting it whitens the roads in puffs like snow round the boles of the eucalyptus trees. Phantoms and Skyhawks train overhead. At Erez is the checkpost for Arabs entering or leaving the strip. In the distance begins the low fence and mine-belt which is the boundary, snaking off into the bare horizon. Gaza taxis are often a beaten-up silvery colour, the upholstery spilling out, and they are overloaded – the passengers stand around listless while somebody opens the bonnet or rummages about in the parcels strung on top. A little scrum of Israeli men and girls are trying to cadge lifts, some just to Mu'azi or Beit Lahia, some as far as the Suez Canal. Mule-drawn carts clop along as though three-tonners hardly existed. And always that slight tightening of the stomach, the prickle of nerves. The green cactus, as modelled as sculpture, never changes. Behind it, on either hand, nothing moves at any speed but there is a pulse to the stillness.

This news story is from the *Jerusalem Post* of 2 November 1971 but it would do for any time these last four years:

Two men wanted by the security authorities were killed in the Gaza Strip on Wednesday, and an Israeli soldier was wounded, in a clash between terrorists and an army patrol. The patrol was conducting a search in the Burej refugee camp when it encountered the terrorists. In the brief exchange which followed, one of the terrorists threw a grenade at the patrol, wounding one of the soldiers. Both the terrorists were killed by fire from the patrol. Personal weapons and grenades were found on their bodies. One of the terrorists was identified as David Halab, who, as a deputy area commander of the Popular Front for the Liberation of Palestine, was high on the wanted list.

A wanted terrorist was shot dead by an Israeli Defence Force patrol in an orange grove near Nazle village, at the northern end of the Gaza Strip, on Friday. The patrol sustained no casualties.

Somebody is seen running, shouts and shots, the whole thing is over so quickly that it is easy to have been here and know nothing of what has happened. Though described as terrorists, even the men on the wanted list rarely use any weapon except a grenade released in the streets. Bystanders, often the children milling around, are the likeliest victims. This is the hit-or-miss affair of an Arab against his enemy, but because it is such a personal gesture its suicidal consequences count for less than performance. In the first four years of occupation in Gaza, 45 Israelis have been killed and 348 wounded, compared to 248 Arabs killed and 1,373 wounded. Out of inexperience, you too roll up the windows of your car and feel watchful, but you soon realize that this grenade-throwing is too undirected to have planned targets; it is less a threat than a way of life like assassination in Cyprus – this is employment and self-expression for those who have been poor and down-trodden for too long to have been aware of anything else.

'The Palestine Citrus Fruit Company'. Beyond this warehouse are the UNRWA offices, still a little outside Gaza City. An elderly watchman is usually sitting by its closed gates, fiddling beads through his fingers. A kilometre to either side is prime terrain for grenades but inside the compound all is quiet, the white UN cars are neatly parked, the huts fresh-painted. Mr Howard Keaney, an Irish-American, is in charge, a tall and quiet-spoken person of the old school. He too has read the newspaper article about Shimon Peres and UNRWA. The more you visit him, the less he has to surmise – Gaza does not change. It was from this office a few years ago that I was first taken to the distribution of monthly rations, of the soap, the 375 grammes of oil, dried beans, ten kilograms of flour to a total of 1,500 calories a day per person. In a sort of super-shed women with tatty cards waited while the lines moved slowly round and the hours idled away. The kind of Scandinavian somehow always present at such occasions was giving tongue. An old Arab answered him, 'This is the face of poverty, my friend, be kind enough to look at it.'

UNRWA has been a local government in tandem with the successive Egyptian and Israeli military authorities; it cares directly for two thirds of the population as registered on its rolls; its staff enjoy privileges of salaries and pensions which truly set them apart. Of the eight camps in the strip, these officials will prefer to display Jebalya and Shati, known also as Beach Camp, because these are the closest. Daily work for UNRWA stops at two o'clock in the afternoon, and Rafah or Khan Yunis are a ninety-minute drive away south, which means a late return. UNRWA has long become a routine operation running in the most fixed of grooves, and since the budget comes from head-quarters in New York and its expenditure has the acutest political sensitivity this may be the only practical course of action. The result is that UNRWA is static, the refugees have been suspended in a permanent present, hand to mouth, and so it may go on and on as the Return recedes and no alternatives are prepared.

The white UNRWA Renault bounces round to the camps. Dust or mud according to the season. At Beach Camp some fishing boats have been hauled in and nets are being repaired. The huts are the basic UNRWA units, in row after row, squared off, half cantonment and half warren. Less has been done than on the West Bank to improve them, and although here and there is a trellis and some good vines, the place in general looks more disregarded. It is the same at Mu'azi or at Jebalya. The UNRWA officials do not like to stop and get down, they point through the window, they look at their watches and tell me that there is no more to it than what I can see.

Once or twice I have returned by myself to Jebalya and set

off from the *souk* to explore. To no purpose. No sooner have I arrived than scores of children materialize out of the side-alleys where they have nothing to do. A Pied Piper procession follows. The grown-ups join in. Ask a question and a multitude of answers breaks out into hubbub. The solution is to attach yourself to someone who will at once invite you into his home, though sometimes that offends the neighbours for they would have liked to do you the same honour – and another crowd jells.

The place has this terrifying mob cosiness. One speaks and all speak. One is ill and all are ill. One throws a grenade, then, presumably on behalf of all, but on that subject nobody has a thing to say. The camp may be a collectivity but at a level which is also a free-for-all.

The Egyptians had created a certain currency turn-over in Gaza, what with its free port, its smuggling and the expenditure of the PLO and UNRWA, but they had held the Gaza Palestinians on a tight rein. Exit visas were hard to come by. Curfews have been continuous for twenty years and in the camps police posts were constructed for surveillance. Out of long habit, each camp at night is silent enough to be uncanny, as though thousands of people had been swallowed without trace into the dark. In December 1969 the Israelis evacuated these police posts because it was considered better to provide fewer targets for possible grenades, and also out of confidence that Gaza Strip developments lagged only six months behind the West Bank's. This was mistaken. In effect the camps were handed over to anyone who cared to rule them, which meant the *fedayeen*. In the main these belonged to the commando branch of Shukeiry's PLO; they had been trained, but scattered during the war. Mostly solo performers, they now had the chance to go beyond grenading and they emerged armed and unpoliced during the day and night in what they had always called their Camps of Liberation. Throughout 1970 the murder rate of Arabs killing one another in the Gaza Strip ran between thirty and forty a month. Whole families were wiped out and, while such murders were claimed to be punishment for collaborating with the Israelis, more often they were a matter of pursuing vendettas and clan quarrels. A number of victims were women who for various reasons had been abandoned by their husbands, and on whom the guerrillas therefore fastened for shelter and alibis. In Jebalya, the *jora* or ditch in the centre of the camp served as a regular dump for corpses.

So in the summer of 1971 the police posts were manned once more and to facilitate patrols of armoured cars, wide swathes were cut through the larger camps. Several hundred houses were demolished and UNRWA officials will point at empty vistas and bulldozed ruts. Sand again. In the end not even misery will have left its scar. Earlier in the year UNRWA and the Israeli administration had resettled about a thousand families into new housing at Nuseirat, Burej and Khan Yunis. But not enough houses had been constructed to take about twice as many again who were displaced in July and August from Beach Camp, Jebalya and Rafah, as a result of these clearances. Some four hundred families occupied abandoned Egyptian houses in El Arish, and fifty more went to the West Bank, while the remainder either moved into rooms they owned elsewhere in the strip, or into other camps, or else simply dispersed. And the murder rate dropped almost to zero.

Nuseirat and Burej are close to one another and are referred to as the Middle Camps. Number of Persons, according to the statistical board in the camp leader's office, 27,897. Number of Nursing Mothers, 936, Number of Pregnant Women, 411, Number of N/H TB Patients, 41. Rations, 25,089. Figures for Public Lats, Private Lats, W/Hand Pumps – this is the mixture of old NAAFI spirit and civil servant pidginese which more than anything has stamped UNRWA. The new houses here were described to me by Shimon Peres as 'not villas but acceptable'. They consist of rooms three metres square, with a larger area of yard. There is running water and a Private Lat and a W/Hand Pump. Outside are the standards for electricity which the Israelis are installing.

In the first of these houses the women are grinding up a fish-meal while the father and son are out working with their mule-cart, to earn a few dollars a day. Eleven members of this family are drawing rations. A carved and hand-painted ottoman chest is in one corner. Next door an old couple live by themselves. The man, barefoot in a *galibiyeh*, is toothless and wizened. His wife is scrubbing the already spotless floor. The neighbours consider that I should not be wasting my time on the life-story of this couple, but visiting them instead. So I do. I sit on a stool. Ten days ago ten houses were demolished here, and three more at Mu'azi, after some *fedayeen* were caught. As matter-of-fact as the weather – and never mind, there are *fedayeen*, there are Jews, and nothing can be done about it – and so many pairs of quick brown eyes search out your face for every inflection.

In Burej village, as in all the villages of the strip, the inhabitants live as they did before the refugees, the Israelis, the Egyptians and even the British, came. Further back than anyone knows, their society has been in collapse, and they are continuing in its ruins. Against the dreads and evils that really matter, they wear amulets and talismans. All are in folk costume. Heavy and superb. Some of them are descendants of black slaves from Africa and have tribal face-tattooing and head-dresses with gold coins sewn in rows. Some decorate pots or weave baskets as their forefathers have always done. How soon are they to live with penicillin and reading textbooks? In such villages there is little or no prospect of access to a doctor or a teacher – what lucky star, what magic, bestowed 1,500 calories a day and a W/Hand Pump on the refugees but not on them? Naturally they use every means of being registered as refugees and it would be heartless not to connive.

Back at the entrance of Gaza City is a Turkish fountain backed by a wall of Koranic inscriptions. Also a fine old mosque. Anything once well-wrought by the hand of man in these surroundings has an almost superstitious power to comfort – life has not always been a process of degradation. Beyond the fountain is el-Wahda Street, half of it demolished in 1965 by the Egyptians to widen the road, which was never in fact done. Fallen arches, more ruins. Parallel to it runs Omar el-Mukhtar Avenue leading to Falestin Square, the centre of the town. One side of the square is taken up by the cemetery and its lumpy graves as though to emphasize that the dividing line between life and death in Gaza is hardly more than a matter of crossing the road. An Israeli half-track is usually still about, lurking alongside the Baptist Hospital perhaps, as on that occasion when a sniper had suddenly opened fire, to send me scurrying with the crowd for cover behind a tombstone.

You need to walk, to buy a souvenir or two, or a drink from the *kharoub* seller. Paintwork is distressed by the salty air. Gaza City is down and out, it offers itself for what it is, making no claims. With some corner of the mind everybody is making rapid calculations of danger, keeping themselves agile in case of a grenade. Greeting people, shopping, you too are somehow being congratulated for coming through. I like the Feras market, the unpretentious booths of the Zeitoun Quarter; I like the primary smells of new-made pastries and vegetables cut an hour ago. Doors open on to huddles of men absorbed in their crafts. A glance upwards, a human warmth. Once in the Sejeiyah Quarter a car-load of Israelis drove by with guns sticking out of the windows. With delight the Arabs pointed this out to me: 'See how afraid they are of us.'

There is a run-down hotel once patronized by the British and which offers a bed at two o'clock for a siesta. In it I ran into a former officer who used to be stationed at Nuseirat in Mandate days before the refugees arrived. He was showing the wife and kids this splendid old dump which unlike the rest of Palestine has not changed a bit since he was a peppy squadron leader. The lavatories in Gaza are the minimal English model shipped out to the colonies, either the Niagara OK or the slightly superior Best Niagara. Like the Turks, the British left behind their plumbing, and in a manner of speaking their inscriptions too, having deposited into living Arabic the two catch-all opinions of several generations on that wasting Mediterranean shore: *houlo bullshit* and *fuqqadem*.

At the end of Omar el-Mukhtar Avenue rises a statue in the realist-heroic mould to the PLO Soldier. Behind it is the Parliament where in a room with a neat cupola Ahmed Shukeiry used to preside over the Palestinian Congresses and the PLO

General Assemblies. A *menorah*, or seven-branched candlestick, is on the walls now, and where the delegates used to sit in varnished wooden pews under the rapid fire of so many speeches is a ping-pong table on which Israeli soldiers slosh about. The building has become the civilian administration. Seeing a pile of suitcases in the courtyard, I assume that I have stumbled on deportations, but it is only the luggage of some seven hundred students off to cross the canal at Ismailia for the academic year in Egypt. A short distance off is the military governor's office and there the pace changes, the telephone is always engaged and you have the impression, peculiar to these places, of being in a family business.

Colonel Liram has been the spokesman through these years of occupation and we launch into the old subjects where we left off last time. The latest quarterly report, as it might be. What about the case of Abu Fahm, a prominent captured guerrilla who died in Gaza prison? Surely, he says, after all these investigations I must by now know the answer – Abu Fahm was ill, he died. Only the Communist newspaper *Al-Ittihad* and its supporters try to make propaganda out of it. In his office Colonel Liram has a portrait of Nasser inherited from the previous regime and in his native Viennese way he repeats a punch-line he had used on me the time before that Nasser was Israel's best friend after Ernest Bevin. Today he has to supervise the students' journey to Ismailia.

I am shown into a waiting-room along with two elderly gentlemen, grandpas really, in uniform, with their revolvers clumsily bumping off a canvas belt. One of them is Mr Tzetzik from the Israeli Ministry of the Interior who has been acting Mayor of Gaza since January when Raghib el-Alami and his council were dismissed. Relinquishing his temporary posting, Mr Tzetzik is about to be congratulated by the governor for the work he has put in hand. In seven months he has been planning and performing on an unprecedented scale: sewage, drains, filters, telephones. The main road has been raised forty centimetres and there will be no more winter flooding. There has been nothing like it perhaps since the Turkish governor who built that fountain.

You wonder how they can go on mustering such energy, such drive, year in year out, warding off the *fuqqadem* outlook. They take it for granted that they will never hear a word of gratitude, and they suspect that the Arabs are right to hold themselves out of reach. In the Arabs' position, most of them would behave like that too. But what else is there for it? In one room after another, with on the walls those happy informal pictures of Palestinian schoolgirls and farmers, the Military Government administrators will lean forward to explain their master plan devised by a committee of economists and sociologists: the big vocational training network; the intended new quarters which will transform the camps. Infrastructure again; the word is their talisman.

In a little official car, white like UNRWA's, an Israeli major performs the guided tour, each time having more to show. The wind cracks along the beach where the port is being built. Ships hitherto have had to be unloaded offshore, the porters often up to their waist in the sea. Unspoilt sand is being churned up by earth-moving equipment, the cement-mixers are spinning. To the north bob the Shati fishermen and overhead drone two helicopters of the coastal patrol. Away from the wharf and the hangars sparkles the clean whitewash of the UN beach-club, a lone Riviera touch. The Red Cross has rented an attractive villa nearby and the Swiss delegate, a tough young man, lets me have a look through the family reunification papers and the across-frontier requests which he has to sort out. Trouble with Arab names, with untraceable people of no address. Part of his job is to see captured *fedayeen* straight after their questioning, and to visit them regularly in Gaza and Ashkelon prisons.

With each stop the major tends to forget his holster under the dashboard. At the Rimal Clinic the new X-ray machine is so expensive that the Ashkelon Hospital doctors have complained because theirs is inferior. The Shifa Hospital would be the envy of Nablus. It has received a large Israeli investment but no Israeli staff. Arab nurses walk past with trays on their heads. Skin

ailments are rife. I notice a mother trying to shove a thermo-
meter through the encrusted dirt of her baby's bottom. On an
upstairs floor is a children's ward where three cases of kwashi-
akor have been treated. A young American nurse had explained
to the mothers that the dramatic cure of the disease consisted
in adding proteins to the child's diet, but they had wanted to
know what fetish the Jews were using. Once, in one of the
general wards, a terrorist had been hunted down, firing from
under a bed. When Mr Peres had come to inspect the modern
wing put up out of his trust funds, the windscreen of his car
was smashed by a brick chucked over the wall the moment his
back was turned.

Overcrowding, malnutrition. No political parties, no newspapers, no institutions, not so much as a football team. The strip
is a slum disguised as an orange grove. Israelis in the administration from General Gazit and portly Mr Tzetzik down to this
major and the devoted civilians in clinics will tell you that the
only solution is to spread the population. But how, and where?
Besides, publicists of the Palestinian cause, who always wanted
the camps cleared, have now changed their minds and defend
the rights of the refugees to stay where they are. Nobody will
leave the camps of their own free will so long as *fedayeen* are
still around to call them traitors and take reprisals. When the
houses in Jebalya and Shati were demolished, families and their
possessions had to be forcibly put into trucks. Pathetic scenes
took place. Israeli soldiers complained against orders to evict
refugees. Back again, then, to compensations and resettlement
at a marginal level. At Tira, a village in Israel, for instance, the
Arabs go to work in nearby Haifa factories and have brought in
labourers from Gaza to till their fields.

The white car deposits you at a canteen which was an
Egyptian officers' mess. A young Negro used to be a waiter here,
and his skilfulness with plates concealed that the fingers of his
left hand had been blown off. The pastime of boys like him in
Gaza was digging about for buried ammunition which sometimes set off explosions, and he smiled about it. A few last
reflections, a final cup of coffee, the major again retrieves his

holster, and off you drive past the battered Amer Cinema and the urchins selling *Maariv* to the soldiers. Outside the UNRWA offices the watchman has removed his chair. Night falls quickly. In the lengthening shadows the banks of cactus look weirder than ever. On the road the blue Egged buses, in convoy one after another, have been returning the Gaza workers from Ashkelon, from Ashdod, from kibbutzim. The windows of the buses have been fitted with wire screens to bounce off any grenade. At the Erez checkpoint more buses are waiting.

The news report from Gaza City in the next morning's *Jerusalem Post* fills in the one out-of-view part of the scene:

Two curfew breakers were shot and killed Sunday evening by an army patrol north of here. The incident took place along the Green Line where the curfew begins at 6.30 pm. The two men were spotted by the patrol and ordered to halt. When they refused, warning shots were fired into the air. But they continued to run, and were felled by bullets.

Another incident, but apparently of no more consequence than the breaking of a wave on the white shore. From dawn onwards the buses have gone trundling to the checkpoint, and Israelis are pleading for their lifts. Gaza is itself. Along with the newspapers I have a press release, *A Declaration from Haj Rashid Said Shawa to the Honourable Inhabitants of Gaza.*

Brothers and Sisters, the long enduring inhabitants of our beloved Gaza. In response to the calls of duty and in realization of your wishes and implementation of your requests as shown in the declaration appearing hereafter in which you have requested me to become Mayor of Gaza and in which you authorized me to choose from among you a Municipal Council to bear with me its historical responsibilities after more than four years of occupation of our beloved Gaza and enduring Strip by the Army of Israel, I have the honour to declare in this announcement that in keeping up with your expectations I have accepted to become your Mayor . . .

Rashid Shawa has indeed been setting to, he has appointed the new Municipal Council which the military governor hastened to endorse. Although in office for just a few days, the mayor has already asked the military governor to withdraw the border police, to release those from Gaza detained for whatever reason at Abu Zneima in Sinai, and to demolish some concrete walls erected to block terrorists throwing grenades out of alleys into Omar el-Mukhtar Avenue.

At the Municipality, a big building overlooking the slender tombstones by Falestin Square, Mr Tzetzik's handiwork is evident in the fresh paint and partitions, the new furnishings and tidier Best Niagara. A clerk is presenting for signature a pile of papers bearing the purple ink-stamp of Israeli bureaucracy. Rashid Shawa is a strongly built man, with black hair, who does not look his age. Half a century ago, his father had been Mayor of Gaza, and the first inhabitant to install a telephone and to own a car. In 1965 a brother, Rashdi Shawa, was mayor during the Sinai campaign and was so maltreated by the Egyptians returning after the Israeli evacuation that he died a few years later – a poor precedent. Rashid Shawa has had some orange-trees destroyed because in one of his orchards a *fedayeen* bunker and weapons' cache was uncovered. But the Israelis have been anxious to have a man of his stature and wealth as mayor. His predecessor, Raghib el-Alami, was concerned with his own business interests. As the concession-holder of the local electricity company, for instance, he refused to link Gaza to the Israeli grid-system. What would serve the citizens of Gaza but lose him some income was then presented in a political slant as a tactic of Israeli occupation. Rashid Shawa is curt about corruption in previous administrations. He calls in the chief accountant and we examine last year's statement to determine what Raghib el-Alami had spent and why there is so large a budgetary reserve. A Municipality like Gaza obviously should borrow and spend all the money it can.

Going through elections for a mayor, however, would have implied accepting the occupation. Direct appointment was also impolitic, but Mr Tzetzik could not stay on secondment for ever. So Rashid Shawa went to Beirut (where his daughter is a most successful painter) and cleared his position with the *fedayeen* organizations. On his return over five thousand citizens signed a petition on his behalf so that his appointment in the end had support from the local establishment, the *fedayeen* abroad and the Israelis – no mean feat, but perhaps an indispensable preliminary for holding one of the least inviting posts in the Middle East.

Terrorists, resettlement, the permanent occupation of Gaza since General Allenby entered it in 1917: we rehearse the *kolubuja* themes. Mahmud Abu Zuluf telephones from Jerusalem. Then Aziz Shehadeh telephones from Ramallah – of all small worlds, this must be one of the smallest. Private business is a public secret. Rashid Shawa likes Shehadeh's ideas and would welcome a Palestinian unity between Gaza and the West Bank, with federation to Jordan. To be returned to Egypt would be a worse alternative, and annexation by Israel the worst.

At least thirty thousand men, in his estimation, or about half the real work-force of Gaza, are finding daily employment in Israel. They see nothing incongruous about it. For the first inconceivable time in their whole lives they are able to bring meat, tins of food, biscuits, shoes, fresh milk, into homes where hitherto everything has been a matter of scrounging and 1,500 UNRWA calories. Terrorism has failed to offer them any alternative. A few grenades exploding into queues of labourers – the worst of them so far causing up to a hundred wounded – are not sufficient deterrents. To the masses, house-to-house searches or identity parades or even detention of innocent passers-by for interrogation after an explosion have not seemed too stiff a price to pay for regular work and all the benefits that go with it. Each crammed Egged bus at Erez is a practical refutation of the guerrillas and their doctrines. If this continues, without a recession, the character of the Gaza Strip will never be quite the same again.

But from the mayor's demeanour how could I have guessed at the extraordinary drama then and there unfolding in his house? For a young man with a Kalatchnikov rifle and a suitcase full of grenades had just pushed his way in one night, and identified himself as Ziad Hussaini, a member of the Hussaini family and leader of the PLO underground in Gaza (there was a

Hussaini Mayor of Gaza in the days of the mufti's abortive All-Palestine Government). He installed himself in the mayor's basement, claiming asylum and hospitality. Then he further offered to provide a list of more than thirty of his accomplices if the Israelis would guarantee them free passage out of the country. There was no way of calculating how the suggestion of such a deal might be received. The mayor had two incompatible obligations. His person and his position were involved in a conflict of duty and honour on the lines of classical high tragedy, which was resolved only when Ziad Hussaini, after lying up in the basement for six weeks, shot himself. A house in which a terrorist is known to have sheltered is blown up, but not in this case because Rashid Shawa's father, it was publicly recalled, had saved the lives of some Jews during one of the Mandate riots by taking them into his house. So his son remains mayor. And the wanted list is much shorter.

Mortagi, Abu Sha'ban, Abu Ghazalal, Surani, there are other notable and respected families in Gaza. The leadership grow oranges, they acquire commercial agencies, they complain about Jewish competition forcing up their labour costs, and above all they stay at home. Plenty of proverbs have been coined on the folly of initiative. In common with their kind all over the Arab world, these last of the effendi class look defeated, as though pessimism were in their skin. Politics here, like terrorism, is a matter of personality, of what sort of figure an individual is to cut. So there is no public life in any recognizable sense, but only one private risk after another and this would debilitate the best and boldest of men. Apathy roosts on the rich and the refugees alike; apathy is safe because no man ever died of it, in this place where something new means something worse.

Gaza College is a private school offering the best education in the strip since its foundation in 1942 by the Tarazi brothers. Wadi'a Tarazi has been Quaker-trained; he is a mild man. The Egyptians always favoured education, and out of a pre-war total of 1,500 pupils they subsidized 300, or rather more than he has now all told. The classrooms are half-empty. On one door a swastika has been chalked into a Star of David. In the office some silver cups for field sports are locked away in a cupboard, the tarnished symbols of other long-ago ideals. In 1969 a demonstration was staged here which the police broke up, and now a surrounding wall has been erected to keep the pupils in. Some have joined the *fedayeen* and from time to time a death among them is reported. A bell rings, school is over. Good-looking boys just growing their first moustache, off they go on foot or on bicycle, out into the town where God knows how many men would like to exploit their basic knowledge of chemistry, to enrol them or to buy them. These days the wanted list has been almost cleared up and here are some more names for it. How are they to arrive at a choice of their own? This is the Rimal District, much of which has been developed these last ten years, quite spaciously by local standards, quite comfortably. At most of these dressed crossroads all the way down to Beach Camp incidents of one kind or another have happened, if only one could pinpoint them by more than the spattered bullet-holes. It is mid-day and within a quarter of an hour nobody is in sight. The sun blinds out the slogans fading on the walls, the sand drifts in curls underfoot.

8 · Courts and Camps

UNRWA headquarters in Beirut are in a former French barracks, yellow-washed and jaunty with old palm-trees. The building suggests a span from today's posters along the streets for Gilbert Bécaud's gala performance at Byblos to choose Miss Lebanon all the way back to spahis and high commissioners stepping from the Residence in the shiniest of cavalry boots. Ask a question from the international civil servants inside and the answer is prompt, probably already printed in a publicity brochure. Their office hours also end at two o'clock in the afternoon, as is the general habit, giving each day an engagingly civilized shape. To save time, it is more convenient to take in the camps around Beirut, but the longer journeys to Sidon or Tyre are at once arranged. Pressingly, unlike in Gaza. 'Thank you for taking an interest in us.' The cliché is uttered in tones of surprise so often that one supposes UNRWA has some house-rule for its employees about it.

Here and there, off the Beirut boulevards, at Shatila, under the umbrella pines of the beautiful deep parks, are the unhoming huddles of any Middle Eastern city. Hutches of corrugated iron, tents strung together, planks, barrels and tyres, all packed and teeming so that to the Westerner, who has only to stand and stare, the human squalor and vigour seem inseparable, but a hard lesson. On one such lot in the city, abruptly, surrounded by apartment houses, live hundreds of Armenians boarded in by a high fence, creating the impression of a giant refuse bin. Near the main market is a *bidonville* of Kurds who are employed as porters, and with a strength and skill beyond any beast of burden they hump upon their backs roped piles of boxes, crates or sacks. What with slops and smells, the place often seems like some fantastic pit into which an undiscriminating power has cast a jumble of minorities: Alawites from Syria, Shiites, Metawalis from the south, the Kurds, migrant peasants off the land, squatters, Bedouin, job-nomads, those whose settled ways have for one reason or another succumbed to modernity.

By comparison a Beirut camp for Palestinians such as Dekwaneh or Burj-el-Barajneh is a village enclave, it has cohesion, it is clean, bourgeois you might say. At Dekwaneh the camp is on private ground and rent has to be paid. Nonetheless the UNRWA shelters have been much improved, second storeys and extensions have been built, television sets and fridges are common. The space between the houses has become an intricacy of steps, corners, crooked alleyways, in a throwback to the classical pattern of an Arab town. In these camps there is the standard dispute about numbers between the camp leader and the UNRWA officials. A lot of refugees come to Beirut to look for jobs, which is illegal, so they cannot then claim UNRWA services. They tend to be either too poor to come forward or too well off to be eligible. If they want rations, they have to return to their own camp where they are registered. Who gets what, who is or is not a squatter, becomes a matter of wits like so much else. Even without a precious permit, it is possible to find a job, or several, and most of the men form a kind of floating labour pool, available for harvest-time, for casual piece-work, for various black markets, all of which will keep them for the best part of the year out of the various coffee-houses playing shesh-besh and cards. Placement boards in the camps advertise openings in Bahrein and Saudi Arabia which the young snap up.

'We Fight Israel Because It Occupies Our Land.' Such slogans, in English, are presumably for the benefit of foreign visitors. The walls are plastered and placarded. 'Public executions in Amman,' a camp leader nods at some photographs which were special press releases but are now duplicated everywhere, showing two young men on the gallows, their heads at that broken angle of supplication but the tongues slightly protruding. The Popular Theatre of some resistance group has posters alongside. On many a wall is the melancholy face with its moustache of Abu Ali Iyad, a Fatah senior commander killed in the Jordan civil war. The refugees muster among these discouraging memorials as in a cemetery.

Dekwaneh has its PLO office. A young man with a sten-gun lounges about, a copy of his Israeli prototype, even in his scruffiness. The sergeant-major is older, more of a veteran; he shakes my hand and explains that his officer is shaving. They have a landrover, painted grey, and only a few days ago its PLO special licence had to be exchanged for regular Lebanese plates with the serial number beginning 499, which apparently is the key to Deuxième Bureau vehicles. Increasing control. They complain of it. The Lebanese Ministry of the Interior contains a Directorate of Palestine Arab Affairs, which used to be responsible within the camps for civilian matters such as movement in and out, while the Deuxième Bureau had charge of security. After the clash in 1969 between the Palestinian organizations and the Lebanese government, an arrangement was reached whereby the *fedayeen* were permitted to operate in the south on the Israeli border in Arkoub, a stamping-ground of fifty square miles which the Lebanese army could supervise. The *fedayeen* in special armed groups known as the Kifah Musallah have since policed the camps where they consider themselves on home base; the Palestinian flag flies there; but the Lebanese government, like the Israeli, has found its way to split the *fedayeen* from the refugee masses.

Jisr-el-Pasha is a small camp precarious on a hillside with a view of the city. It is one of three camps for Christians, it has a social centre, and receives help for its schools and church from the Pontifical Mission. The housing is better, because it was accepted as reintegration and built at a moment when UNRWA had the funds. Those who missed the chance for betterment never had another – that's the history of the Arabs, as a camp assistant says, not too sure whether to be pleased or sorry about it. A photograph of a man is pinned to a door, of his own house apparently, as another memorial, for he was killed down in Arkoub though nobody knows or perhaps likes to tell whether by the Israelis or the Lebanese or the *fedayeen*. They are explaining their tricky relations with the Kifah Musallah, who are Moslems, when we hear shots crackling close at hand. Soon some young men with automatic weapons come in sight, and they are far too nervous for us to stay for cross-questioning by them, or so the driver insists, hurrying us away in the big UNRWA Dodge. The young men stand morosely gesticulating.

In one camp after another this sense of strain and suspicion is more shadowy than in Gaza but unmistakably signalled. Under the Palestinian flag the Kifah Musallah watchpost may belong to one of many organizations, Fatah, PFLP, PLO, the Iraqi-sponsored Liberation Front or the Syrian-sponsored Saiqa, bidding for power separately or in combination. Para-military figures, a blockhouse, a machine-gun behind sandbags on a flat roof: is this an assertion of command over the refugees who live within the field of fire below, or of strength against the Deuxième Bureau and the Lebanese army? Nobody rushes round to talk. Even *kolubuja* and hopes of the Return sound muted. The UNRWA officials and camp leaders here will tell you that the Palestinians are after a bigger revolution than simply going back to what they were before, and something like that means keeping the most careful of look-outs.

One of them accompanies us to Nahr-el-Bared, a camp a few kilometres from Syria and susceptible to whatever crosses that frontier. To get there, we have driven up the long coast into Tripoli whose new housing looks as if it had been bodily transplanted from Israel. Tripoli provides the political base of Rashid Karami, formerly prime minister, and pro-Palestinian. The refugees cannot vote but they may be induced usefully to rush down Rashid Karami Boulevard demonstrating against the Moqqadem family who are the rivals of Karami and his party, or openly rioting so that a change of government in Beirut becomes necessary. During the *fedayeen* heyday, Tripoli was a turbulent city. The roads to Nahr-el-Bared were cut in August 1969 when the *fedayeen* took control of the camps. The

Lebanese Army quit, the Kifah Musallah took over. Then the Cairo agreements were implemented and now the army and the Palestinian Kifah Musallah, PLO soldiers mostly, cooperate without much friction in running the camp.

In a sandy compound close to the seashore bamboos lean in as windbreakers, UNRWA ration trucks are being unloaded. The Kifah Musallah men come to inspect us, followed by other *fedayeen* from various groups. We sit around a table, we stare at one another. The argument grows heated: I may be allowed only to drive around, or perhaps go on foot, in which case the market will be out of bounds; I may not speak to anybody. Finally we set off in a party of about ten, as if I were a duty-officer with an escort, but also a captive of circumstances. And nobody so much as catches my eye as they go about their business in the *souk*. I feel invisible. I learn that only a day or two ago a boat with four *fedayeen* set off from here for Gaza, but was seized as it entered Israeli waters. The people here are convinced that there must be a traitor in their midst. I hear myself beginning to say that a traitor is less to the point than the Israeli coastal patrol and their helicopters hovering up the Gaza Strip – but the implications suddenly link me to that feeling of invisibility.

Not far off, at Beddaoui, is a training ground for Lion Cubs, more like a sports field really, with the jumps and frames of a miniature assault course. A couple of kilometres away, the camp was sited among surrounding orchards in 1956 after the local river in flood had swept through the previous UNRWA shelters and it now has claims to be the nicest in Lebanon or anywhere. In the camp leader's room is pinned up the photograph of prisoners at Kfar Yona which had illustrated my article on the subject. Its caption says, 'Take your hands off our students.' Outside a tubby fellow in a red beret is playing with the safety catch of his automatic rifle; he is from the Iraqi-sponsored Liberation Front. The PLO centre is near a handcrafts workshop – the conflict to get either tools or weapons into a man's hand is immediate. And on the way back, in Tripoli, down in the Mena Quarter by the old harbour where we stop to buy fish, the driver takes me on one side to say that over a hundred families from Nahr-el-Bared and probably as many again from Beddaoui have just spent the summer on the West Bank and I am not to believe a word of this morning's fighting talk, it has been a charade for my benefit. Why, he himself is from Jaffa and the worst mistake of his life was to take his brother's advice in 1948 and leave. Next year in Israel, he promises, just like any Zionist. Offshore two big oil tankers are anchored. Past the IPC terminal with its huge storage tanks and pipework is a golf-course, unexpectedly green. At length we are dropped for lunch at the New Yacht Club out of Beirut. The boats are spick and span on the brilliant water. The season is already past, there will be no more outings in the bay, no more water-skiing. Down by the quay Cadillacs and chauffeurs are in line. In the dining-room Butrus el-Khoury, a well-known Lebanese financier, is entertaining friends. The head waiter is all attention. The shaded terrace gives on to the wonderful sweep of the coastal mountain with its absorbing variety of architecture, old and new. And after such typical experiences any day in the refugee camps, every visitor and every reporter, Arab or European, radical or not, mixes guilt down with a great deal more than 1,500 calories.

'The people from Fatah will come for you at 1900 hours.' Indifferently the concierge at the hotel desk hands over the message. As he has done so many times before to so many other anticipating journalists these last two years. In a great gold-and-glass room off the main hall a society wedding reception is taking place, the women strikingly beautiful in this year's Balenciaga and Balmain, sequins and diamonds, with sheafs of white flowers everywhere. Those Lebanese who can afford it have nothing to learn about luxury from their former French mentors, or from anybody. In fact the people from Fatah do not come. Since the Jordanian civil war, the *fedayeen* organizations have become more random about appointments, more conspiratorial, or possibly more on the run. Spokesmen are no longer on call, they are on some secret mission, they are away in Arkoub, they refer to others and provide telephone numbers which do not reply. The lists of useless numbers accumulate, and mornings can be dissipated trying to dial them. Yet Beirut is the centre in the Middle East for a number of foreign correspondents and the battle for publicity is such that they cannot be entirely dismissed. The little knot of newsmen must have addresses to go to, and more doors to knock on, further lists of telephone numbers to ring. The German camera-crew and their student interpreter, the Swedish Trotskyist and his Belgian chum, the English Arabist in his tropical suit too rumpled to show dandruff and stains from the one-too-many *arak* – can these really be the arbiters of Western public opinion? With reason, Palestinian activists resent the way they have been taken up, inflated, and dropped. Whose fault is it if they are a nine days' wonder on the tenth day?

The PLO office is in a universal-Bauhaus squared block of a building on the Corniche Mazraa, an important thoroughfare. A Palestinian flag waves over the entrance. On the first floors the doors bang as scowling young men hurry in and out with what looks like factitious mid-morning urgency. Another floor up are piles of packing-cases stamped in heavy black lettering in English from the Russian Embassy, Beirut, and these serve as wonderfully suggestive stage-props for the bug-eyed German television team. Beyond are the rooms of the PLO figureheads like Kemal Nasser and Shafik al-Hout. Coffee is served with the greatest courtesy, someone called Jamal says that the exact relationship of the PLO and Fatah for the present is indefinable. The PLO and Fatah comprise eleven groups, well really eight, or actually a core of three, and its Executive Committee is composed of – somehow there is always an interruption, a tapering-off, to these organizational discussions. Factionalism and jockeying for place reveal the latest adjustments in higher Arab politics as well as the dependence of the Palestinian movement on patronage. After a while the attempt is abandoned to sort out which countries have subsidized which groups at which moments for what purposes.

In a cul-de-sac on the far side of the Corniche are the offices of *Al-Hadaf*, weekly magazine of the PFLP, and in a way its headquarters since George Habash and Wadi Haddad virtually went to ground after the Jordanian civil war. The eagle emblem of the American Consulate stands in one corner as a trophy after some demonstration, and it is balanced by an Israeli bomb-casing. The paper's editor, Hassan Kanafani, is articulate and so much interviewed that his political beliefs have come to do for the PFLP's. As a Marxist–Leninist he will say that the Palestinian resistance movement has four enemies, imperialism, colonialism, Zionism, and Arab reactionaries, or in other words everybody in sight. The struggle is part of a historical necessity and though it therefore cannot collapse, its bad periods have to be survived. (A few months later he was to be assassinated.)

As for the PDF, which broke away towards ideas of permanent revolution, for the time being it is in disintegration. Naif Hawatmeh and its leaders are in Iraq, and supporters, who were never more than a few hundred at most, are searching for explanatory texts. Its paper *Al-Hurriya* is suspended while the editor and the staff sort out a doctrinal dispute. The PDF's position becomes increasingly a series of personal statements. Mutual recriminations cancel each other out. One man after another claims that his organization or outlook alone is blameless and uncompromised, the others being deserters or opportunists.

As in so many previous movements of the kind, the main split is between nationalism and ideology. Nationalist elements such as Fatah and the PLO would like the recovery of Palestine to be an absolute end in itself, to which all means should be subordinated. Once the military objective is achieved, in short, politics may break out. Ideological elements like the PFLP and PDF want an Arab revolutionary and socialist world in which Palestine will take its place. It is the chicken-and-egg riddle in another form: which comes first in order to give birth to the other, Arab socialism or the recovery of Palestine?

Long-term strategy and short-term tactics depend on the thrusts of this dispute which could be resolved only by the creation of a real unitary National Front. It seems that Fatah were advised by Algeria to achieve such a thing even if it meant murdering all their ideological opponents. And indeed the Beirut newspapers do publish many stories of false identities and forged documents, of kidnapping and assassination between Fatah, the PLO and other groups, which their partisans waive as exclusively internal affairs. However murky an action looks, the political context can be made to cover it. Left-wing illusionists versus right-wing revisionists, in the angry jargon which is bandied about. None of this mutual labelling does justice to the situation in that it diverts the primary cause against Israel into secondary but no less lethal quarrels. The material pinned to the various office walls – as in the refugee camps – indicate which opinions are to be studied and obeyed. Everywhere are photographs to inspire militancy, of guerrillas on the warpath, each man shrouded into the secrecy of his *keffiyeh* but brandishing a gun. The best of these action-shots have been mounted on board and are exactly the reverse of the peaceful images of Palestinians which those Israeli administrators are trying to cultivate on their side of the divide. Ideology is more simply a matter of Mao and Guevara, although North Korean support for the PFLP has added a touch of Kim Il-Sung. You might as well be in a Black Panther or La Raza or Fourth International stronghold anywhere in America. Such conformity is probably because so many Palestinian students have done their undergraduate course in sociology or politics on the campus.

In *Eothen* Kinglake invented a celebrated dialogue between a traveller from England and a pasha. Guying them as a couple of representative specimens, he relieves himself of what must have been a lot of repetitious stuff. The pasha had just become acquainted with the Industrial Revolution: 'I know all . . . my mind comprehends locomotives. The armies of the English ride upon the vapours of boiling cauldrons, and their horses are flaming coals! Whir! whir! all by wheels! – whiz! whiz! all by steam!'

Nationalism in this century is whatever the Industrial Revolution was in the last by way of a European wonder to the rest of the world. Kinglake's traveller today might hear from a Palestinian activist something like this:

The PLO and its army never get off their behinds. Fatah are basically Moslem Brothers, that's their appeal. They also picked up one of Nasser's insights that whatever a mob does, at the end of the day it has to go home. The PFLP think hijacking TWA planes publicizes the cause when it reveals only the complete inability to hit Israel. All the organizations reflect simply the disarray of the Arab world. So Feisal pays Fatah, and Iraq pays Hawatmeh. All are petits-bourgeois who want good safe jobs and hidden accounts. Never mind. The revolution is far bigger than them. What except the revolutionary movement as a whole can claim to represent the Palestinians? Certainly not King Hussein after his Black September. He lost that battle by winning it. The Israelis? They may convince themselves and perhaps others too that they are democratic but objectively they are reactionary. Whatever they do on the West Bank is wrong, that's what occupation means. So it's the Americans, is it, with Israel and Jordan both tied to them as twin monsters to their mother? You read about their conspiracies in books like Miles Copeland's and *The Pentagon Papers?* There will be *coups.* One day Syria or Egypt will have an Arab Castro. The Americans would no doubt unleash Israel or Jordan against an Arab Castro. But radical change is bound to come by radical means. The national movement is now irreversible, we are in the first stage of the people's war. Forces will be more and more crystallized. Look at Gaza! The fact is we aren't Red Indians. We read Zionist papers, we know the contradictions at work over there. And the military instrument is only the violent form of politics.

Whir! whir! all by revolution – whiz! whiz! all by liberation.

The Palestine Research Centre and the Institute of Palestine Studies have both been founded within the last ten years. The former is on Nazlat Karakas, a small square not far from the smart shops of Hamra Street, and the latter is within walking distance of the university. Both places aim to present the Palestinian case in its own right but also by an exposition of Zionism. Some competition exists between them. *Palestine Affairs* is published by the centre and the journal's last number had interviews with George Habash and Khaled Hassan, the head of the political section of Fatah. *Palestine Studies* is put out by the institute. The centre is promoted by the PLO and it is closer than the institute to the rough-house of politics, but the staffs of both places have those close if nebulous links with the *fedayeen* which escape the outsider. In the corridors are displayed photographs and maps which switch the issue over the centuries with some caption like this one: 'As far back as 2500 BC Semitic Groups from the Heart of the Arab Desert Migrated to Egypt, Iraq, Palestine, Syria and Lebanon.' On several desks lies the annual Palestine Diary, every page of which carries some reminder of *kolubuja*, a pinch of salt to rub into the wound of each day. (Flicking through, I find some of the best poems of Rashid Hussein whom I knew ten years ago in his village of Musmus, just inside Israel in the Little Triangle, as a teacher and member of the neo-Marxist Mapam Party before joining a Palestinian organization in New York. Now I dare not admit that within the month I have been in Musmus to pay my respects in his absence.)

In both libraries are files of the *Jerusalem Post*, *El-Quds*, *El-Anba* and *Al-Ittihad*, and indeed all necessary research material in Arabic, Hebrew or European languages. Several Israeli–Arabs are employed here, and also some one-time *fedayeen*, like Ahmed Khalifa of the PFLP, who have learnt Hebrew during a spell in an Israeli prison. Such evidence on the subject as they have to give has long been put before one commission after another (the latest has recently been sitting in the five-star Phoenicia Hotel) and if it does not quite tally, it is mostly less assertive and extreme than what you can hear inside the actual prisons. In these quieter surroundings, stories of torturing tend to be reduced to a matter of having been shoved upstairs or awoken roughly in the middle of the night to answer the same questions continuously. One of these former prisoners asked me to imagine what it was like for him, an Arab brought up in a decent family, to be cursed at by the toughest of Sephardi Jews. Most of the young men are students or graduates, and even without first-hand experience they have a pretty clear idea of what the West Bank occupation is really like. To their credit they are able to face the consequences – individually they are likely to say that Palestinian resistance has come to a dead-end for the present. But even if nothing can be done about Israel, they would argue that it is still essential to study the enemy informatively and not simply give way to superior force.

The books and pamphlets under the imprint of the institute or the Research Centre are organized, edited and written by the handful of Palestinian intellectuals who all along have borne responsibility for fuelling the cause's fire – Anis Sayegh, himself Director of the Research Centre, and his brothers Yusuf (Chairman of the PLO Planning Committee) and Fayez who come from Tiberias; Walid Khalidi, a member of the old Jerusalem family, and a most incisive speaker and writer; Hisham Sharabi, Abdel Wahab Qayyali who is also a publisher, Henry Cattan, Sami Hadawi. Some of them also teach at the American University of Beirut where their colleagues include other prominent Palestinian professors and authors, Nabil Shaath, Ibrahim Ibrahim, Halim Barakat, Mahmud Zayid. At AUB, that most appealing of campuses, with its halls called after American missionaries, Nicely, Ada Dodge, Bliss, another generation of students has to be measured against the fixed conceptions of their elders.

The Palestinian orbit revolves round such men and their activities, their articles, their television appearances in America and Europe by special invitation and on condition that their Zionist counterparts do not sit in the same studio, their platform addresses and debates at Arab universities and congresses. They are an elite on their own terms in Beirut, they meet in the salons of the more socially-minded *fedayeen* sympathizers and hostesses, or at weekends in the mountain villages where they may have a country retreat, they see one another as they have been doing since childhood. They know what there is to be known of everyone else's public and private doings. They know with what spirit of nationalism Wadi Haddad's father once taught Arabic studies at St Luke's School in Haifa. They know about Habash's parents in Lydda, and about the embittering death of his sister from typhoid during the panic of 1948, and also in whose flat he is concealed today. They know how Ahmed Khatib joined with Yasser Arafat in the early 1950s in Kuwait, and who was in the Arab National Society at what point, and who has made sacrifices for their beliefs and who has made money instead. The past is ever-present to them. So close to their Garden of Eden but forbidden from it. The older ones like to recall when some of their best friends and neighbours were Jews who never dreamed of becoming Israelis – a thought which works powerfully on those who know about Israel only from books. Coming as they do, by and large, from the former educated classes of Palestine, they share in a style of aloofness, almost disdain, rather as some Central European aristocrats do in their exile. Public militancy may screen private resignation, but underneath any postures they may have, their sincerity and affliction are equally unmistakeable. They send their sons to camp with the Lion Cubs and their wives to help with good works for the refugees, in voluntary associations or propaganda outlets like the Fifth of June Society.

Too intelligent to ignore the coexistence on the West Bank, these intellectuals have also experienced the gulf between them and the refugees in the camps. Always they have felt guilty over their dereliction in leaving Palestine in the first place, but more so now than ever, when they would have wished to be setting an example under enemy occupation and not phrase-mongering in safe and idle Beirut. Out of the Palestinian cause they may make a living and a reputation while the ordinary refugee, should he even want to show solidarity, has the likely prospect of earning little more than his memorial photograph ragged and wind-blown on the walls of his camp. Israelis have smashed their past, Arabs have squandered their promise, and their lives are poisoned. So they complain about work-permits, about the bureaucracy which cramps and controls them in Lebanon, Syria, Jordan, Libya, everywhere, and about the unpopularity which hits them in the face. The more they complain, the more unpopular they become, the worse the controls grow, in a circle which is closing smaller and tighter. No success in a professional career is compensation enough. Talks and meetings, parties even, fume away into the saddest of silences. Jewish intellectuals in nineteenth-century Russia and Poland, theoretically but not in practice emancipated, must have experienced just the same helplessness as they consoled themselves with Zionism.

1900 hours again, and I am escorted to a Fatah office in the Daouk Building on Ardati Street. Big and badly lit. No indication that it is not an ordinary apartment. A double knock on the door. Inside several youths have nothing much to do. In berets, they give the impression of being in uniform. A balding man with spectacles and a girl in a mauve sweater explain the posters and give an account of the death of Abu Ali Iyad, Abu Sabri and other September victims. On Abu Omar's desk are files marked Armed Struggle, and Jordan. Abu Omar says that 983 *fedayeen* and 2,000 Bedouin were killed in the civil war – generally estimates are five or six times greater. Personal questions cannot be answered, and of himself Abu Omar says only that he was born in Haifa, left as a small child, and is a cadre of Fatah. An exceptionally good-looking man, he is in American gear of tight trousers and patent leather shoes to suit his American accent. On his wrist is a silver bracelet. A blending of the physical and the intellectual. He quotes Fanon but sticks to the well-used slogans. He hands out pamphlets. I cannot be allowed down to Arkoub to see the Fatah in the field, it would be too much of a security risk. Fatah has three schools and he will arrange a visit.

In the rain-sodden night Beirut shines, its electricity a pearly blur. Car tyres squeal. Headlights along the Corniche. That Fatah office had something reassuring about it, the sense of an exclusive club-house for like-minded friends to retreat into for a way of life sheltered from the city outside and the hard sea crashing on the esplanade rocks. A tourist boat has docked, the night-clubs and red-light spots will be crowded as the passengers succumb to the charms and resilience of Beirut, the possible setting, still now, for a cosmopolitan novel as Alexandria once was. According to the taxi-driver, King Hussein owns this high-rise block and King Feisal that one over there. Money from the Gulf ends up in these skyscrapers. And posters from everywhere have ended up in Abu Omar's room, posters of Angolan guerrillas, of Biafra and Bangladesh and the Black Panthers and Ulster, in the ginchy colours of fashion design the world over. Politics as commerce – those posters promise that there is a guerrilla group perfectly made to fit you too. Going along to Abu Omar's for the evening is buying yourself in with the right group as much as sitting in 'Sweet Sixteen' or a topless joint with the boat-passengers.

Next morning's *Daily Star* has a gossip-column. 'After Dark: A terrific dinner party at Nobs and Carl Petersen's penthouse pad in the Daouk Building had the group of all-nighters dancing away after a superb dinner of prime rib roast and everything that goes with it.' That double knock on the door, but nobody has taken steps to organize a visit to the school. Abu Omar is away, having been up all night apparently (upstairs chez Nobs and Carl?). At length a student is spare. Having caught a cold in the changeable weather, he sniffles into a handkerchief. Another taxi-ride, past the office of *Al-Hawadess*, one of the several good Lebanese papers, past a discreet sign to a Palestine Red Crescent clinic for Fatah, on to the main road to the airport. So around the curves and loops up the mountain behind Beirut, to Bmakkin where the nuns are, past the Hotel Hajjar, to the village of Souk-el-Gharb.

'The School To Make Children Happy'. Its sign is painted over the entrance. The building is somewhat bleak, though practical, put up in 1958 by the General Association of Palestinian Women but bought by Fatah two years ago with funds from Algeria and China and Kuwait and Saudi Arabia. Its 250 pupils have just about doubled in number since the September events in Jordan. Almost all of them are orphans between the ages of two and thirteen, the children of the martyrs of the revolution, as the director and the student-guide call them. A good many of them are disturbed, it seems; they are too young to know their names, they weep at night for their mothers. The student is a serious, unemotional type and says that he is blowing into his handkerchief only because he has a cold.

The Lebanese curriculum is followed but the children have

additional hours of indoctrination on politics and Palestine according to the level of their class. In the director's words, they are to be the revolution of today, and the generation of victory. Boys do sports with a para-military emphasis, and if they are poor at studying they transfer to the Lion Cubs. In one classroom girls are copying out big rolls of banner-slogans about the Third Extraordinary Congress of Jordanian-Palestinian Students at the refugee camp of Ein-el-Helwi, and the proposed Jordanian National Front. One of these girls, about nine years old, puts her hand into mine and will not let go; she does the whole tour. She clings. In the dormitories the beds are heart-rendingly tidy, the cupboards virtually bare of possessions. Through the wide windows over the tops of the pines is a view of Beirut clustered far below, with the sun sparkling on it and the sea widening into the blue mist of the distance, a sight none of the children will be forgetting.

Landings and rooms have been named after Nazareth, Tiberias, Jaffa, Ramleh, Jerusalem, and everywhere hang en-larged photographs of these towns as they were before 1948, as though the Israeli hand had never touched them. Reality may not obtrude. The places have been sacramentalized. Should any of the children ever be returning to Palestine, they will never recognize where they are. No portraits of Arafat or any leaders are visible, no personality cult is fostered. Only the cause in the abstract. To mention refugees in camps is to be slightly dis-paraging. In this cleansed and rather Spartan austerity, these orphans are the fortunate ones for whom the school lives up to the sign over its entrance. All that is asked in return is sacrifice.

A crest or two farther along the mountain lies Shemlan, a picturesque village which in summer is something of a resort. Ahmed Shukeiry has come to retire here in a large white house which is shut for six months while he winters in Cairo. Recently Shukeiry has published a volume of memoirs resonantly entitled *Dialogues and Secrets with Kings.* 'Admittedly, I frequently called on Arabs to liquidate the State of Israel and to throw the Jews into the sea. I said this because I was – and still am – convinced that there is no solution other than the elimination of the State of Israel and the expulsion of all Palestine Jews from Palestine.'

On the road off to Brumana lives Haj Amin, once the Mufti of Jerusalem, frail and in seclusion. Visitors are scarcely welcome. Those who led the struggle for the cause have been broken by it, and have almost broken the cause. Shukeiry, the aged mufti, the Fatah school and its children too, are castaways in this region. As another minority they may sink or swim. Nobody has a good word for the Palestinians, not in these Druze or Christian or even Moslem villages, not behind the high stone walls of the villas and park-like gardens, nor hardly in Beirut itself, either among ordinary Lebanese or among the rich and powerful, the Eddés and Gemayels, Chamouns, Franjiehs, Salems, those who are themselves nationalists and fill the high offices of state. In their eyes, Palestinians represent trouble. Palestinians are to be blamed for the destructive intrigues which led to General Bustani's dismissal from the army. Blamed also for the scandals of Yusuf Beidas and his Intra Bank, or of Adrian Jday who went to prison for share-dealings in the Casino du Liban. To them, Palestinians are a threat to tourism, business and stability, being either a charge on the public or else fanatics who provide a standing pretext for an Israeli raid – though the *fedayeen* fire more shots within the country than across the border. If Lebanon is not to go the way of Jordan or be bust open once again into civil war along confessional and sectarian lines, the Palestinians have to be put in their place by the army.

'You want to go to Arkoub and see.' The taxi-driver has taken scores of correspondents down, he bumps off on to short-cuts and side-roads past the road-blocks. He has friends everywhere. Southwards the country is wilder, more scenic than ever, ideal for walking and camping. We arrive near Bint Jbail, to a place where the driver stops and as proud as any proprietor, displays the hills towards Mount Hermon which the Israelis know as Fatahstan. Plenty of woods, unlike in the Jordan valley. In the distance, high and a little shadowy, is Israel. The afternoon softens. Enough is enough for the driver, who gestures towards another of the many hillside villages from which the *fedayeen* must be observing all movement. Until now, he has been claiming to be on the best of terms with the commanders of the region, but apparently he does not want to be put to the test. Somewhere below us the Israelis have laid a link road entirely on Lebanese territory and they patrol it regularly, they have posted intelligence officers at known spots to which the villagers come with news and denunciations of the *fedayeen*. In effect the Lebanese have contrived for the Israelis to do their police work for them. On the west the Lebanese army, on the east the Syrians, box in and narrow the scope of what is the last terrain available to armed Palestinians. Every so often *fedayeen* cross the frontier ahead and fire a Katyusha rocket into Kiryat Shmoneh or a kibbutz or at a passing car. Another Israeli is injured or killed. An Israeli column retaliates up that road and houses are demolished in some village as the price for having *fedayeen* quartered there. During the few days after such a foray the Israeli intelligence officers receive more information than usual because everybody knows that prevention is better than cure. In a repetition of what happened in the Jordan valley, probably half the Arkoub villagers or more have fled to be out of harm's way, though they will return if there is calm. For the best of reasons, the *fedayeen* have obtained the worst of results. Like other bands of the self-elected, they punish those whom they hoped to save.

9 · The Verge of Jordan

Behind the Place des Canons in the Bourj, or what remains of the old part of Beirut, my fellow-travellers have already assembled, all four Palestinians as it happens. One of them, a youngish man with a cheerful smile and an armful of newspapers, has bought a new antenna for his car, one so long that it is an awkward bendy piece of luggage. Rightly he foresees how many forms will have to be filled in for it, what entries on his passport, what deposits paid. The officials between Beirut and Amman need not speak to make plain their assumption that a radio antenna of this size must be communicating to the KGB and the CIA before the day is out.

Syria has Welcome signs and billboards in Russian since I was last here some eight years ago. Traffic is overwhelmingly military. More new barracks, more soldiers, more women and girls in the uniform of this or that social pioneering brigade. You have the sense of stumbling upon some semi-balkanized province under the pall of the north, although Damascus with its ancient glories and a certain modern spaciousness has always somehow remained inviolate. On the outskirts the same UNRWA housing or tell-tale *bidonvilles* give away the presence of refugees. In fact more refugees live in Syria than in Lebanon but far fewer of them are in camps, having been better integrated without inter-denominational strains. Political considerations apart, Syria could absorb every Palestinian and more, for as a Roman province it supported a much larger population than it does today, and was still exporting grain.

The antenna is transferred to another car, and we take our

places. To the south the road opens on to the flat and lonely roll of the Hauran plain with its basaltic stones as black and numinous as cairns. At the Sheikh Miskin crossroads Kuneitra is indicated – the Israelis are about thirty minutes away overland. A policeman stops us, gets in and has himself driven down to Deraa. Nobody has a comment to pass until we are rid of him. 'The Bey wants you.' It was in Deraa that Lawrence heard this sinister order and whatever really did happen to him there, 'that night the citadel of my integrity had been irrevocably lost'. Somewhere around the town the PLO army is stationed, and with it the Palestinian elements which deserted from the Jordanian army during the September fighting, though they have no more independence of action than if they were the few extra kilometers across the Jordanian border.

There, at Ramtha, a Bedouin corporal spreads out on the ground my possessions including a bulky collection of Palestinian resistance literature, in wrappings luckily, but which, it strikes me much too late, is subversive and banned. But the car antenna comes into its own, the young man is led away for cross-questioning, the corporal is distracted from tearing open Black September pamphlets given to me by Abu Omar and others. The Bedouin have been trained on spit-and-polish, and they carry swaggersticks with a brass bullet mounted on one end. The usual mislaid Western hippy squats in the dust with his flowing karma robes and sandals, to the limitless scorn of the groomed soldiers. The hippy says that he is too timeless to bother about paperwork. He and the Bedouin might be doing cabaret skits of one another. At last the young man is released with his car antenna from the flurry of the police post. Nameless humiliations have made him white in the face, unsmiling, tight-lipped, but he is only one among four of His Majesty's most disloyal subjects to pass through the army searches and road-blocks all the way into Amman.

Not only Deraa but the whole of Transjordan, its elephant-hide hills and parched wadis, has had thrown over it the veil of imagination. Adventure. *Seven Pillars of Wisdom* may be disliked and its faults are obvious, but it is not an immaterial book.

Lawrence is the country's unseen guide. Tafileh, Kerak, Aqaba, the desert: whatever towns and mud-huts and tents exist in reality, still they have had put on them the stamp of a great literary fantasia. There is something preservative and a little intimidating about it, in this unyielding sunlight and rockiness of Jordan – a glint that every mark once made on the landscape for better or worse will never be changed.

The extraordinary Victorian travellers and soldiers like Charles Conder, Sir Charles Wilson, Sir Charles Warren, usually out on behalf of the Palestine Exploration Fund, had first recorded the region's imposing splendours and aridities, as well as typically classifying certain asphodels or Tristram's grackle, a bird unique to the Dead Sea. Sometimes they had nothing but ill to say of the Bedouin who were only nominally under Turkish rule, but tribal divisions and genealogical complexities between the Beni Sakhr, the Howeitat, Anizeh, Adwan, Shammar, Ruwwala, appealed to their English curiosity and delight in other people's customs. Also they liked to suppose that they had left the Bedouin as they had found them, implying that the encounter had been between equals, a sentiment which was sometimes genuine but always myth-producing. Every traveller is creating his own epic around himself. Lawrence had his vision of the Bedouin forming a unified nation-state like any other, and of his own leading role in the process. This vision, if successfully fulfilled, as it has been partially, could only mean the end of Bedouin life as it was. Lawrence's successors in the field, like Kirkbride, Somerset, Colonel Newcombe, Peake Pasha, by and large followed the same course, busily and devotedly administering out of existence what they most valued.

The purest elegiac summary of the change and loss comes from Glubb Pasha, the last of this colonial line. In his memoirs *A Soldier With The Arabs* he writes,

The last Bedouin raid occurred in June 1932. I spent nine of the happiest years of my life, from 1930 to 1939, as officer commanding the desert area. Nearly three quarters of the area of Transjordan was desert, though the Bedouin population amounted only to some fifty thousand souls. I deeply loved these poor simple people and became so intimate with them that among them I felt as if I were at home. From 1932 to 1948 the whole of Jordan was indeed one of the happiest little countries in the world ... how many Transjordanians have said to me since then with a sigh – 'we were so happy until 1948.'

Until they were a nation-state, in short, with other nation-states all around, just as raw and uncertain. 'Worse was to come.' These words crop up like a refrain in King Hussein's *Uneasy Lies The Head*, in which he summarizes some of the unhappiness of his reign.

A century ago Amman was a collection of tents for Circassians cantoned there by their Turkish overlords. Today it has up to 400,000 inhabitants, three quarters of them Palestinians, who have indeed built the city up, though in the main they would rather have been elsewhere. Only about one in four of the refugees on the East Bank lives in camps but altogether the Palestinians make up an urban population, and in that respect they are non-tribal, as opposed to the Bedouin. Charles Doughty, the most eccentric and courageous of English explorers in Arabia, once had encamped at Ramtha on his way south with the *haj* at a time when only the Circassians were at Amman. 'Great is all townsmen's dread of the Bedouin, as if they were the demons of this wild waste earth,' he wrote. The comment applies today. The September massacre is how Palestinians will talk of the civil war, treating it as a tribal razzia of pillage, rape and murder in the old desert style. A blood-letting. In their eyes the Bedouin are backward, ignorant and corrupt, taking money from whoever will pay for whatever purpose. Transjordanians, or Bedouin (not always the same thing), will say that the Palestinians were too weak and cowardly to fight the Jews, so ungratefully they turned on their hosts and brothers. Press and television, all of it controlled, put the accent on the Royal Council of the Tribes, on tradition and desert lore and martial virtue, propagating the idea that the Bedouin are all that is best and truest and most hard-core in the Arab world. This is useful sentimentality, however, for during the years in which the government has been relying on the Bedouin for its loyal soldiers it has been settling them on the land and sinking wells for them, educating them as much as possible, and in fact detribalizing them and modernizing to mutual advantage, as the British administrators once used to do. To be stopped at any road-block where Bedouin soldiers are searching Palestinians is to experience the ancient antipathies between tribal men and town-dwellers in their newly acquired dressings.

Since the civil war, the army is in absolute command. Of the *fedayeen* nothing active remains. Their offices, once so thronged and courted, are abandoned, padlocked as like as not. In the event the various *fedayeen* organizations proved to have owned, rented or commandeered an unexpected number of top-floor flats, with roofs which offered a field of fire and an ultimate defence – mostly bullet-scarred now, unless already repaired. Here and there stands a blackened ruin. On Philadelphia Street, a short distance away from the spot where the Israeli tank-driver rode on in his death, is a gutted apartment building. No more Fatah jeeps shooting traffic lights under the eyes of a policeman wilting at his post. No more strong-arm squads raising voluntary funds or imposing and collecting obligatory sales taxes on food sold in the market. No more posters, no more faces of the dead, no Abu Ali Iyad, for instance, bringing down revenge on his memory. These absences, these silences, are eloquent. Everybody has his story to tell of that September, of curfews and the nightly fusillades and alarms – which did not stop until the guerrillas were finally driven out of the country the following July. Here is a friend who did not go out of doors for ten days, not even when a bazooka shell wrecked his kitchen. Another friend was trying to save his books when some *fedayeen* rushed in, held him back and started firing out of his living-room windows.

Setting off in the morning to drive where you like induces the wariness of an unwarranted liberty. The roads to Jerash and Ajloun look unnaturally empty, where once the *fedayeen* used to stop cars and demand authorizations. Sometimes spent shell-cases are dumped, presumably for collection. No more hillside bivouacs either. At one village near Ajloun, the PFLP had put into application the ideas of Chairman Mao and they had lived with the peasants, instructing them in ploughing, building, collectivizing. A mind-and-heart operation. And now those same villagers are eager to show off the cave where they trapped the last five PFLP men, killed and decapitated them. Is it true, one wonders, or are they hoping to work a passage into other minds and other hearts?

Where the side-road winds into Jerash camp, a checkpoint has been set up. One of the Bedouin security guards is taking a pot-shot at a big bird across the field. The olive-trees have been burnt to stumps. During the fighting the great majority of the people here fled to hide where they could, just as they had scattered off the West Bank and then out of the Jordan valley at the time of Karameh. About ten men and women were killed and twenty-six housing units razed. Artillery was directed on to one or two of the larger buildings like the Distribution Centre. The camp leader's board has bullet-holes in it, and so do the tin sheet-walls of the police post. A discussion starts. One of the assistants says that the only people to join the *fedayeen* were those who had never seen five dinars in their life. Such recruits should never have been accepted. The *fedayeen* were decent men who had meant well but they caused trouble, they did not think out what they had been trying to do. For instance they had expected the camps to rise in revolt behind them in September, and that could never have happened. The man lapses into gloom, everybody nods, and we walk away rather fast as if he had committed himself too far.

The Fatah tent with its ping-pong table has gone without trace. In the last two years an impressive amount of buildings have been put up. The government and UNRWA have pushed on with emergency programmes. Instead of tents, the concrete prefabs stand neatly. An important delegation from the World Health Organization and UNRWA, complete with medical inspectors and area officers, happens just to be passing through. With their hands clasped behind their backs they are asking the right questions, receiving the right statistical replies, and through them I catch the echo of my own voice. On the ground outside the Supplementary Feeding Centre a madman is rocking himself from side to side. His head has been shaved all over, he is stripped to the waist and fat enough to be blubbery. He shouts and shouts but nobody pays any attention.

Outside Baqa'a is a new American contraption, the Satellite Tracking Station, which raises its parabola high into the sky like a vast blank face, suitably inhuman considering that a few hundred yards away about 40,000 DPs are living without electricity. This emergency camp, like the others, has been trans-formed. The disaster-zone which I remember from my last visit has given way to a planned settlement, to chlorinated water, refuse collection, delousing and bath-houses. The hysteria has also ebbed. The *fedayeen* tried to dislodge the people in September, a *mukhtar* says, as we sit in his house. When the army arrived, he was one of those who negotiated with them: the *fedayeen* would be handed over if two trucks were provided for transport and if the army stayed out of the camp. But the inhabitants of Baqa'a had also marched down the road towards Amman until they were stopped. They had shouted, 'We're going to Musa Dayan in Jerusalem.' This is a recurrent trailor of apocalypse in which all Palestinians converge on Israel in a long biblical-type exodus, harassed first by Arab governments and then either mown down at the borders by the Israelis or transcendentally overwhelming them. It is a civilian version of the *fedayeen* death-or-glory wishfulness.

In a hut in one of these brown cement rows a woman is roast-ing some nuts on a kerosene stove. Her sister helps. Eleven children between them, two rooms to sleep in, no pairs of shoes. The husband is a house-painter from a village somewhere on the coast, and he has work tomorrow. One of the baby boys urinates on the floor, splashing the family bedding. Not for the first time. According to the house-painter, as he draws up stools for us, nobody here really thinks that they will ever return to Palestine; they should never have left, they had no reason to, they want a second chance, and he pleads like a schoolchild punished for something he cannot understand. He would like to see what has happened to his village. The *mukhtar* and the painter sigh, and the women roasting nuts appear angry because I refuse to stay and eat with them. Next door there is the same meekness, the same passivity without end, and in the hut after that, and in the following row.

Also at Hussein camp, at Schneller, up at Irbid. As in the Gaza Strip this is a life in which an old oil drum whacked flat is a worthwhile possession because it is better than nothing. The basic class distinctions are between rotted teeth, black teeth and gold teeth. There is neither the will nor the means to change it. Everybody has done the best they could, and more. The camps are cleaner, healthier, renovated in a way that nobody seeing them in 1968 could have anticipated. No doubt it is also the case, as UNRWA and government officials say, that the refugees should not be accepted at face value. They are treated as ordinary Jordanian citizens and for the most part they work, though not regularly; they find openings and they have their small tricks and ploys like burying their dead under their huts for fear of losing a ration-card. They get a plot of land somewhere and somehow build a house on it to let while they live rent-free in a camp with education and medicine thrown in. They have lots of babies. Some make good. Yet such considerations lose their impact before the apparent evidence of eyes and ears, as the days and the questions waste perpetually into one another.

Since it was established in 1952, Wahdat has become a part of Amman, it has a general market, it has grown from 9,000 to 41,000 people, and used to be known as 'the Republic of Palestine'. On the opening day of the September fighting, the army tried to enter the camp but suffered so many casualties that it withdrew. Artillery was brought up. The inhabitants escaped into the city. Apparently it came as a surprise to the camp's defenders that life-long refugees should run off like that. George Habash had his PFLP headquarters there and in Wahdat he had confined the last handful of hostages who had been hijacked off international flights a few days previously, to find themselves unwittingly at the centre of a larger drama. The place where they were kept is pointed out, and a good hide-out it must have been too, although so flimsy that a single direct hit from a field gun would have killed everybody inside. In the 1950s Habash and Haddad had started a free clinic on Jebel Webdeh nearby and they are gratefully recalled for that – 'perfect gentlemen', the phrase goes for them too.

A revolutionary committee of *fedayeen* ran everything in Wahdat until the Bedouin finally stormed the camp. We tour what was a real battlefield, rebuilt though much of it is, except for bullet-marks. Back in the office of the camp leader, Abu Nabil, four women are quarrelling over a conduit to be laid outside their houses. A neighbour is upset. Someone has lost face. Blows have been exchanged. We listen, we try to get to the bottom of it. 'You are seeing it for yourself,' an official says. 'Everyone is fed up, and so am I.'

Earlier in the summer I had been at Schönau, a dilapidated country *schloss* in a once-splendid park of oaks, south-east of Vienna. It has been a night-club but now it is the reception centre for Jews who have managed to emigrate from Russia to Israel. Such a turn of events was beyond prediction. At Schönau it is a question of counting heads. One by one, family by family, they have risked everything to come for a new start, according to the tenets of classical Zionism. With the Palestinians in their camps it is still the opposite approach of all-or-nothing. Palestinian refugees have become a sort of special-interest group, for others to treat of them in the plural; they are the extended family whom nobody wants but will buy off if there is nothing else for it.

Whatever the rights of the Israelis, Arabs once possessed Palestine. Whatever the rights of the Arabs, Israelis now possess it. Instead of ghettoes, these camps. Instead of an identity, a diaspora. 'Our hope is not yet lost to return to the land of our fathers.' So begins the Israeli national anthem but its sentiment is Palestinian. But any new state for them would have to be at Jordan's or Israel's expense. The subject revolves, like history itself, looking for a solution, for a moral. The refugees remain where they are. The UNRWA men talk about numbers and budgets. Abu Nabil chases the four women away with a final threat of the police. They huffily draw their shawls round their faces. Some builders arrive about roofing. Shouting, and patter, and too many people doing too little.

If the 100,000 DPs who left their farms in the Jordan valley after the battle of Karameh would only return and begin productive work again, immediate prospects would improve. The government encourages them, it promises them aid to re-build. Before the civil war, a journey into the valley would have depended on the *fedayeen* and the presence of an escort clatter-ing with his sub-machine-gun all the way down to whatever had been arranged for the press. Nobody goes now.

Halfway down the winding wriggling road is Salt, the capital before Amman grew to its present size. King Abdullah's former low-fronted palace has been made into a school. Many of the town's old streets are too narrow for anything larger than a donkey. The houses stand close enough up the hillside to shade each other. Bits of Roman statuary and Crusader stone have been incorporated wholesale into them. A Lawrentian idyll would be to retire here and devote a lifetime to Arabic studies. The Israeli Mystères and the *fedayeen* between them are simply the latest to have passed over and left their craters and scorch-marks on the stony surrounding slopes.

Under the arches of an old stone bridge a blitzed vehicle is rusting. Bamboo shoots are feathering along the sinuous bed of a stream towards the Jordan. In thunderclouds of diesel exhaust, heavy-duty trucks from the West Bank grind uphill continu-ously, a few no longer bothering to remove the licence plate with its Israeli lettering which gives away their origin. The Allenby Bridge is ahead. Abandoned, the village and camp of Karameh have crumbled, past repair, a counterpart to Aqabat Jaber nest-ling in the purplish shadows of the bluffs across the river. Ruin speaks to ruin. At the centre of Karameh stood a monument to the *fedayeen* and it too has been broken. Junk everywhere, holes, waste. A lieutenant appears and we clamber up to the roof of a house. At our backs are a few new housing units to lure the farmers again into the rich untilled fields. About a dozen men have collected downstairs in a makeshift shop, all of them old except for a boy. The hours are long. No cars pass. The farmers will return, they say, if they feel safe. Why not? Nobody talks much down here unless they have to. Dust sticks to the clothes. In July the last of the *fedayeen*, a hundred of them in all, crossed the river a little north of here and gave themselves over to the Israelis. That was the end. The old men and the lieutenant point out the Israeli positions, visible to the naked eye. They shrug. Flies buzz on our hands and faces. Heat. Lassitude. Silence.

Everybody knows Miss Winifred Coate. Born in 1893 Miss Coate has lived in Egypt, but she is one of those English people whom Palestine has captivated. In some ways she is the spirit of the British Mandate. A teacher for the Church Missionary Society, until 1948 she was headmistress of the English High School for Girls at Rehavia, in Jerusalem. In 1948 the refugees who came to Jordan and finished up at Zerqa had nobody to raise a finger for them; they lived in calamity conditions. Miss Coate arrived. For eight months she could distribute only UNICEF powdered milk. Then she got going. She moved into a house opposite Zerqa camp, started a clinic and an embroidery workshop and won a contract from Glubb Pasha for army uniforms. Machines and textiles were shipped from England. When Glubb was sacked, the contract stopped.

In 1961 Miss Coate bought 1,500 dunams of desert at Abdeliyyah, and the governnent allocated her 500 more. This land is within sight of Ksar Halabet, an Omayyid hunting-lodge which had once supported a considerable number of people, and therefore, Miss Coate deduced, must have had water. The government declared that there was no water. Miss Coate found a water diviner and together they went dowsing. King Hussein himself opened the first of their four wells. Now Miss Coate has fifty men and their families employed on fifty plots, and after paying fifty dinars a year for ten years they will be the owners of the title deeds of their land and house. According to their capacity they also pay for water and fertilizer.

Miss Coate's grey hair is cropped short. She is wearing a green tweed suit and strong brogue shoes. Her talk is of geological surveys and the government test pump and how to deal with the impossible land registry. A fair's fair, nanny-knows-best manner. Her Palestinian partners take me out to the project, as she calls it, out on the road to Mafrak. The Iraqi soldiers who entered the country for the Six-Day War used to be stationed here in a string of barracks until they returned home after the September fighting in which they were mysteriously inactive – it was the third time since 1948 that Iraqi forces had entered and left Jordan. At Wadi Dallal, just opposite Abdeliyyah, the well-known Mu'ashir family have taken inspiration from Miss Coate and farm thousands of dunams, but on a share-cropping basis. The king's uncle, Sherif Nasser Ben Jamil, and Wasfi Tel have also done the same with estates away across the dunes.

As a result of Miss Coate and her dowser the desert blooms. From a central office at Abdeliyyah radiate dusty roads picked out with cypresses now well grown. Water for irrigation is carried alongside in cement channels. Just out of sight is Dawson's Field where the PFLP brought down their three hijacked airliners and sparked off the civil war. The peasants like to show how they ducked as the huge planes swept over their heads. After the million-dollar explosions, the Bedouin picked clean most of the scrap but not all. On the skyline Ksar Halabet is clear and jagged in this time-defying light. The uplift at such hard work and success among the refugees is as sudden as the desert wind shaking the cypresses. 'Poor things,' Miss Coate had said, 'they'll never go home and they know it.' If they did though, they could sell these farms and have a bit of capital. A subsidy of two months of the oil-income of Libya, for instance, and the whole Palestine problem could be solved along these lines. But even the money which is promised to the Palestinians is not paid. The latest *fedayeen* delegations set off to Peking or Moscow or Jeddah or Dar-es-Salaam or wherever each week the rainbow appears to end. Meanwhile Miss Coate is studying the latest catalogues of mechanical engineering equipment to have come in the post.

Some of those who have run foul of the Israelis have set up shop in Amman. Loyalists like Ruhi Khatib, ex-Mayor of Jerusalem, are more than welcome. Ideologists such as Ibrahim Bakr or Rushdi Shahin make common cause with the fragmented groups of left-wingers. Ba'athists and former putschists in opposition, many of them from well-off Christian families in Kerak, Maadaba and Salt, who hope that Communism will dilute the Islamic and Moslem Brotherhood spirit in the air. In the main, their line is to recover the West Bank, which for once coincides with official government policy and so long as that lasts they will be tolerated.

Whole sections of more bourgeois Palestinians (to use the approved parlance), do not suppose that struggling against Israel or the recovery of the West Bank have much to do with the Palestine resistance organizations as such. Since 1948 their lot has been thrown in with Jordan where they have families, property and careers. The *fedayeen* threatened their existence. Before the civil war it was expedient to string along with them and pay up. Perhaps the Republic of Palestine would finally be not a few shacks over in Wahdat but the whole requisitioned East Bank, with the Hashemites disposed of on the Iraqi model, or else away in Geneva or Portugal with other royalty. Neither the king nor the Fatah leadership wanted a bloody confrontation, but neither could predict accurately the reactions or the popularity in a show-down of PFLP extremists, or Communists, claiming as they did, to have the refugee camps behind them. In the political drift it was essential to reinvest against every possible future.

By virtue of their prominence in the community (as well as by inclination) several millionaire Palestinians like Abdel Majid Shuman from Beit Hanina and the founder of the Arab Bank, or Farid Said of the Jordan Tobacco Company, made public their strong nationalistic opinions. The size of their contributions to *fedayeen* of one group or another was a subject of rumour. Beyond a certain point, they lay themselves and their fortunes open to reprisal from the government; they could be accused of financing subversion. What such people really thought cannot be determined by what apparently they said or did. Their dilemma was as sharp as if they had been on the West Bank. The penalty for miscalculation could be destitution or possibly death. Fathers who were in government or otherwise prominently in view were fortunate if they could spread allegiances by having one son with Fatah and another writing PFLP publicity in Beirut and a third safe in Canada, or still more irreproachably in an Israeli prison. This might cut the other way, of course, as in cases like Sheikh Ali Ja'abari of Hebron whose son works in Amman and could have his father's deeds visited upon him there. When it came to fighting in September, the last-ditch refuge was the West Bank itself. Even so committed a politician as Ibrahim Bakr was prepared to send his family to shelter out the storm under the Israelis.

Who knows who is an agent, or double-agent, or on whose behalf, in this twilight of bribes and violence? Once an attack on a police post by an unknown splinter group of guerrillas led by Taha Dablan was the signal for a government crack-down. A provocation, or a real attack? Taha Dablan is in prison. Are there really good and bad *fedayeen*, as the government likes to distinguish them? In August 1970 in broad daylight, in front of the Intercontinental Hotel, some armed men kidnapped Selim Sherif, a rich man in the newspaper business, who had been a partner of Mahmud Abu Zuluf in the old days. Two years later Selim Sherif's clothes are still stored in the Intercontinental, nobody has identified the kidnappers, nobody says whether Selim Sherif is alive or dead. In the Shmisani district of Amman stands a big new building in a slightly strange neo-windowless style, looking like the home of a medium-sized American concern. The grapevine says that indeed this was put into operation by the Americans, for it is the new security headquarters, the province of Mohamed Rasoul.

Since that September, Palestinian civil servants, diplomats and executives have been under pressure, they have had to trim, sometimes to resign. As a precaution Palestinian officers in the army have been denied promotion to senior rank, or superannuated. The technical corps like artillery, services, signalling, are largely recruited from Palestinians and their loyalty to the government was a disappointment to the *fedayeen* as well as one of the keys to the civil war. The newspaper *Falestin* became *Al-Destour*, on the insistence of Wasfi Tel, so it is said. To receive public funds the Palestine Hospital would have to change its name. The West Bank itself is called literally Al-Dafa Gharbiya, and not Palestine. On many a desk, in many an office and shop, a colour photograph of the king has newly appeared, while stories of meetings with Arafat are not repeated. To cooperate or not, and if so, how much, that is the crunch for Palestinians, on the East Bank as on the West Bank.

Some of the great stone villas of Amman recall Jerusalem, but on a larger and richer scale. In the formal rooms of these houses around Second and Third Circles or on Zahran Street where the queen mother lives, and also Sherif Nasser Ben Jamil in his sumptuous orientalized palace, and Akif el-Faiz (present head of a clan whom Lawrence once called all mad), take place the cabals and fine adjustments. Depending on the hour's need for militancy or pacification, prime ministers and cabinets are picked among the restricted range of politicians – the king may call on whom he pleases. The mere mention of their names brings out stock responses about what they will do. Several Palestinians are of ministerial rank. Ahmed Tuqan (elder brother of Fadwa in Nablus) has been prime minister and is a close adviser to the king. Mohamed Daoud, also Palestinian, briefly headed a military government at the start of the civil war (and when he died recently his coffin went from Amman for burial in Jerusalem with the Israelis taking over military honours from the Arab Legion at the bridge). Proposals for the Palestinians in the end lie somewhere with this handful of influential men, in the absence of other representatives. Whatever emerges is known at once to the traditional leaders on the West Bank, and without much further delay to the Israelis and the *fedayeen*, for all of it is connected but unfinished business.

The prime minister's office was surrounded with guards, as well it might be, for Wasfi Tel epitomized the fears and suspicions of

Palestinians. Blood was on his head, supposedly, for however many Palestinians had died in September. He was accused of being willing to make a settlement with the Israelis, of not wanting back the West Bank with its half million and more Palestinians to add to Jordan's disruption. He was from Irbid and again was thought to have called for revenge on the guerrillas from the moment they took control of his home town in the civil war and held its governor a captive. Yet as a young man just out of AUB, Wasfi Tel had worked for the Palestine cause in Musa Alami's Arab Office (and had married Musa Alami's former wife). He was thickset and handsome with black hair and a moustache, looking like the Arab ideal of a warrior. On the backs of his hands were blue tattooed patterns. The room in which he worked was book-lined, it had a comfortable sofa. He wasted no words on the intricacies of the West Bank and the prospects of peace and war. The attitudes of the *fedayeen* had made head-on fighting inevitable. Nobody who had lived through those days would wish to see them again.

Worse was to come. Before that week was out, Wasfi Tel had been murdered in the lobby of a Cairo hotel by four Palestinians. They shot him at midday in the open, the way King Abdullah had been shot twenty years before, as though the death of a prime minister or a king could be thrown into a balance to redress a lost nation. But long ago the feud had become personalized. One of the killers on his knees licked at the victim's wounds. 'Your blood we shall drink and we shall not pity you.' To himself he might have been acting out the lines of Fadwa Tuqan's poem: 'As all the people awoke and arose and said: Revenge!'

Index

173

Index

Index

Index